COUPLES
IN TREATMENT
Techniques and Approaches
for Effective Practice

COUPLES IN TREATMENT

Techniques and Approaches for Effective Practice

GERALD R. WEEKS, Ph.D.
STEPHEN TREAT, D.Min.

Marriage Council of Philadelphia, Inc.
Division of Family Study
University of Pennsylvania
School of Medicine

BRUNNER/MAZEL, *Publishers.* • NEW YORK

Library of Congress Cataloging-in-Publication Data
Weeks, Gerald R.
  Couples in treatment : techniques and approaches for effective
  practice / Gerald R. Weeks, Stephen Treat.
    p.   cm.
  Includes bibliographical references and index.
  ISBN 0-87630-678-4
  1. Marital psychotherapy.   I. Treat, Stephen,
II. Title.
RC488.5.W44   1992
616.89'156—dc20   92-10047
                                                                 CIP

Published by
BRUNNER/MAZEL, INC.
19 Union Square West
New York, New York 10003

Manufactured in the United States of America

10   9   8   7   6   5   4   3   2

Dedicated to

KATHY WEEKS
and
ELIZABETH TREAT

to whom we are committed
in marriage with all of its
problems, promises, and pleasures

Contents

Preface

The purpose of this book is to present some of the basic techniques, methods, and strategies needed by the couples therapist. In a previous volume, Weeks (1989) presented a theoretical approach to couples therapy and provided an overview of the structure and process of treatment. The current book moves to the next step, which is that of providing the "how to." In this book only enough theory is given to make sense of the techniques which follow.

The authors of this book both teach and supervise postdegree trainees at the Marriage Council of Philadelphia/Division of Family Study, University of Pennsylvania, School of Medicine. This experience has taught us the need to provide clinicians with skills that have broad applicability and can be readily used. The skills described in this book are simple, straightforward, and foundational for couples work. Advanced skills, unorthodox techniques, and techniques with limited applicability have been purposely excluded. For this reason, the text is ideal for the beginning couples therapist and as a review volume for the seasoned couples therapist. Over the years we have refined these methods in order to make them teachable and usable, and unlike other texts, we discuss in detail the implementation of the techniques.

Another unique feature of this book is the emphasis on couples growth and not just problem resolution. Many couples therapists assume that by eliminating problems they will enhance the intimacy of the couple. Our approach is to focus on both goals simultaneously— problem resolution with enhanced intimacy. By adding this dimension to couples therapy, the process is enriched for both the therapist and the couple.

CHAPTER OVERVIEW

Chapter 1 describes the comprehensive treatment of the couple using the Intersystem Model. This assessment enables the clinician to formulate a multileveled treatment plan. The chapter also discusses some of the common mistakes made during the evaluation phase and provides suggestions to avoid these pitfalls.

Chapter 2 discusses principles that will enhance the ability of a couple to use the therapeutic process effectively. General topic areas are: expectations and myths; boundary issues such as lateness, fees, and missed appointments; and instruction on how to help a couple take responsibility for their growth.

Chapter 3 covers the importance of balance in systemic therapies. Several techniques for a balanced approach to individual partners in dyadic therapy are discussed. Included are: client understanding of balance; inclusive language; intensity and balance; and seating arrangement to promote balance. Understanding psychopharmacology and balance; determining whether balance has been established; and loss of balance as an important area for personal insight conclude the chapter.

Chapter 4 contrasts linear thinking and interventions with a systemic perspective. The difficulties many beginning therapists have in learning to think systemically are elaborated through the descriptions of a number of systemic interventions.

Chapter 5 covers the challenges of learning to listen to the content of a client communication while understanding and being sensitive to the process. Content and process are defined and contrasted. Methods of understanding the process of a therapeutic session are enumerated.

Chapter 6 orients the reader to skills of building intensity and relatedness within a therapeutic session. Approaches to building intensity and emotional expression, as well as learning to manage them for the couple are discussed. The use of images and analogies, a description of specific interventions to raise emotion, use of repetition, and the importance of focus on primary themes and material are the main topic areas.

Chapter 7 discusses the use of systemic intervention when counseling an individual member of a marital dyad or committed relationship. Issues of balance, empathy, self-responsibility, and the development of personal power are emphasized.

Chapter 8 provides a growth-orientated model for the clinician based on a clinically useful theory of love. Techniques to enhance intimacy are suggested for the couple who want to move beyond a problem-focused therapy and the underlying fears of intimacy which generate many problems.

Chapter 9 covers one of the most generic of all therapeutic techniques used with couples. Reframing is a technique used to change the meaning of symptomatic behavior from negative to positive and to change the couple from seeing their problem as individual to one of relationship.

Chapter 10 offers a framework for teaching couples how to communicate more effectively. A general framework is used to teach couples different levels of communication, specific techniques are reviewed, and communication problems are elucidated.

Chapter 11 addresses the issues of anger and conflict as inevitable in all relationships. This chapter examines anger as a constructive emotion which has many underlying emotional components. A teachable conflict resolution model is outlined.

Chapter 12 reviews a largely ignored area of couples therapy. How and what partners think—their cognitions—are examined with an emphasis on common cognitive distortions. A systemic model for using cognitive therapy is described.

Chapter 13 focuses on three methods of contracting that couples may use to help renegotiate their relationship. Ways of implementing and maintaining contracts are also discussed.

Chapter 14 follows the cognitive and behavioral chapters with a discussion of feelings. The authors describe techniques to help identify and express emotions as well as to manage feeling in the session.

Chapter 15 covers the subject of homework. All of the techniques in the volume may be extended to such practice at home. This chapter discusses how to give homework, identifies the structural elements of a homework assignment, and offers suggestions to increase the compliance to doing homework.

Acknowledgments

In the early 1980s, Mr. Bernie Mazel, then President of Brunner/Mazel Publishers, asked if we would be interested in writing a book describing the Marriage Council of Philadelphia's course in Couples Therapy. The staff of Marriage Council wrote one book that was published in 1989. It was written for the seasoned couples therapist and did not represent our beginning level course.

Inspired by Mr. Mazel's suggestions, we wrote *Couples in Treatment: Techniques and Approaches for Effective Practice*. Writing this volume has led us to appreciate how much our students have taught us about what is usable, and often used, by the beginning therapist. We not only teach, but also supervise students, and it is they who have helped us recognize what the beginning couples therapist needs to learn in the long trek to becoming a master therapist.

We want to thank four of our colleagues for their careful editing, helpful suggestions, and constant support. Joellyn Ross, Rick Mack, Bea Hollander, Shirley Jacoby, and Larry Hof were always there when we needed them.

Liz Clark did much of the typing and provided the needed organizational skills to keep the project on track. Her attention to detail was superb, and her humor always a delight.

Introduction

The development of the systems theories and therapies has represented a major paradigmatic shift in psychotherapy. These new therapies all represent a shift away from the individual and intrapsychic theories developed and employed by Freud and the psychoanalytic/dynamic therapists. The systems theories all share the concept of the individual-as-part-of-a-system and they focus on interpersonal variables.

The past 20 years have been the "systems era" in the history of psychotherapy. In this short period of time, eight major schools have developed, which Kaslow (1981) has grouped under the following headings: (a) psychodynamic-psychoanalytic; (b) Bowenian; (c) relational or contextual; (d) experiential; (e) structural; (f) communication-interaction; (g) strategic-systemic; and (h) behavioral.

These schools of thought all share some basic assumptions about the nature of dysfunction and treatment, but they are clearly different in content. In fact, these schools of therapy were originally presented as if each was to be used exclusively, without "cross-fertilization" from others (see Gurman & Kniskern, 1981a). However, most practitioners of systems therapy and others who are not systems oriented do not operate from such a purist basis. They recognize the implicit need to fit the theories to their clients rather than fitting the client to a single theoretical approach.

This clinical need for integration has led to a new effort within the systems approaches. The latest development, one which spans approximately the last nine years, is toward the integration of intrapsychically and interpersonally oriented theories and the integration of the various systems theories. A number of papers have been published advocating the synthesis or integration of various theories. Many of these papers have moved thinking within the field towards developing models of how different, sometimes apparently mutually exclusive, theories and therapies can be combined. For example, Kaslow (1981) published one of the earliest papers advocating a diaclectic approach to family therapy, in which practitioners can draw "selectively and eclectically" from various theories.

Duhl and Duhl (1981) presented one of the first clinically integrated models which they called "integrative family therapy." They looked at all the levels of the system, for example, developmental level, individual process, transactional patterns. Their approach was focused primarily on how the therapist thinks and intervenes and was less concerned with theoretical discussion regarding how theories could be integrated. The next year two papers appeared which discussed how systems theories could be integrated. Berman, Lief, and Williams (1981), senior members of the Marriage Council, published a chapter on marital interaction, in which they described principles of marital interaction and also discussed how several theories could be integrated therapeutically. In this paper, they succeeded in presenting a coherent way of combining contract theory, object-relations theory, multigenerational theory, systems theory, and behavioral analysis all within a developmental and therapeutic model.

In addition, a number of other articles and books have appeared which address the issue of integration in systems therapy. These include: Hatcher (1978) on blending gestalt and family therapy; Abroms (1981) on the interface between medical psychiatry and family therapy; Stanton (1981) on how to integrate the structural and strategic school; Green and Kolevzon (1982) on convergence and divergence in family therapy; Levant (1984) on a classification scheme for different theories; Lebow (1984) on the advantages of integrative approaches; a series of articles on the integration of structural-strategic therapy edited by Fraser (1984); Doherty, Colangelo, Green, and Hoffman (1985) on ways of reconceptualizing structure and distance in integration; Wachtel and Wachtel (1986) on designing intervention strategies based on family dynamics in individual therapy; Weeks and Hof (1987) on integrating sex and marital therapy; and Weeks (1989) on integrating individual, interactional, and intergenerational approaches.

THE INTERSYSTEM MODEL

At the Marriage Council of Philadelphia, the approach we have developed to treating couples is known as the Intersystem Model (Weeks, 1989). This approach is comprehensive, integrative, and contextual.

Whenever a couple is being treated, we believe three systems or subsystems must be simultaneously considered: the individual, the interactional, and the intergenerational. Most other approaches to marital and family therapy focus only on one or two of these systems, whereas we have found an integrative approach requires focus on all three. Perhaps our most striking departure from other systems approaches is our focus on the couple as a system consisting of two individuals. Other systems approaches have for the most part been anti-individual and antidiagnostic in the traditional sense. Unfortunately, systems thinkers have been so intent on separating or differentiating themselves from individual approaches that they have totally discarded the value of seeing the individual as an individual. In our approach the individual's coping mechanisms, defense mechanisms, life cycles, ethnicity, intrapsychic dynamics, and individual psychopathology are assessed and treated within this context, rather than denying that individuals exist in such contexts.

Obviously, the couple's interactional system must also be assessed and treated, because a couple is more than the sum of its parts. Couples develop spoken and unspoken contracts, communication styles, patterns of dealing with or avoiding conflict, and so on, and the interactional system is usually the first experience a therapist has with a couple. This system is always present and the easiest to observe. The third part of the couple is the intergenerational system. Each member of the couple has a unique history rooted in the family of origin. These experiences, historical and current, influence the current relationship. In many cases, couples re-create unresolved issues with their own parents or previous relationships using their partner or children as a substitute. Consequently, intergenerational influences are often hidden until an exploratory process uncovers them.

The purpose of this book is to help the reader conceptualize and treat the couple from multiple perspectives and with a multitude of techniques. We do not advocate any single approach to couples therapy. The therapy should be crafted for the couple *and* their problem(s). Techniques can be sequenced and blended in order to tackle different problems and problems at different depths. The techniques described in this volume are not advanced or complex. They are basic techniques with wide-ranging applicability and power to effect change.

PART I

BASIC PRINCIPLES OF COUPLES THERAPY

Chapter 1

Assessment and Treatment Plan Formulation

In order to use the techniques presented in this book effectively, it is necessary to conduct an assessment of the couple and develop a formulation of the case. The assessment phase consists of the initial interview and four to five more sessions. This chapter will not focus on the details of how to conduct these initial sessions because this aspect of treatment has been adequately covered elsewhere (see Haley, 1976; Heller, 1987; Weber, McKeever, & McDaniel, 1985). Heller is a colleague of ours, and thus her article is especially representative of our approach.

Our ideas for case formulation stem directly from the Intersystem Approach developed by Weeks and colleagues (1987, 1989) at the Marriage Council of Philadelphia. We advocate an assessment approach that is comprehensive, multidimensional, multilayered, which will allow for comprehensive, multidimensional, and multilayered treatment. Many case formulations in our field are based on a single theory, which means the couple is conceptualized and treated within narrow parameters. This fact exists because many practitioners tend to adhere to just one model of intervention. As we have indicated, the field is becoming more theoretically and technically integrated. In a previous book, Weeks (1989) stressed theoretical integration; this volume stresses technical integration or the use of techniques from different approaches.

Before describing how to develop this type of case formulation, we would like to give the reader some guidelines on how to get started with the assessment phase of treatment. These guidelines are framed in terms of don'ts and do's, and are designed to help the clinician avoid some of the common mistakes which are made.

COMMON MISTAKES MADE IN THE EVALUATION PHASE

The evaluation phase of couples therapy usually requires two to four meetings. During these meetings the therapist's task is to join with the couple, collect information needed to develop a case formulation, and avoid mistakes which would disrupt development of a therapeutic relationship. The first two tasks mentioned above have been discussed widely in the literature. With the exception of Haley (1976), little attention has been given to describing the typical mistakes a couples therapist might make which can abruptly end treatment. The purpose of this section is to list some of the don'ts and do's which are so important during this phase. Many of these ideas apply throughout treatment. However, once the therapist has established a relationship with a couple, a mistake does not have as much potential to result in premature termination. The couple is more likely to be forgiving and discuss mistakes openly with the therapist. Although we call this list don'ts and do's, the reader should view them as useful guidelines and not as dogma.

Don'ts and Do's

1. *Don't take sides.* It is easy to get seduced into taking one partner's side, especially when the other partner's pathology or contribution to the problem is not as clearly evident. The therapist must keep a systemic perspective. Otherwise, the partner being sided against is unlikely to return, and the accusing partner has his or her linear view of the situation reinforced. The therapist should shift back and forth trying to understand each partner's perspective. The way the therapist uses language during this phase is important. The therapist needs to use reflective listening and use phrases such as "It is your perception, belief, opinion, idea, thinking, and so on." For example, the therapist should say "It is your perception that your wife is controlling" rather than "Your wife controls much of your behavior." The latter statement implies that the therapist agrees with the validity of the statement being made.

2. *Don't intervene too quickly.* The therapist may feel obligated to start changing the system before understanding it. Premature intervention may destabilize the couple in such a way that it is too threatening for them. It is best to go slowly and intervene in ways that

appear safe or nonthreatening to the couple. The task is to join and collect information early on in treatment. The couple can be told the first few sessions will be to conduct the evaluation and then to develop a treatment plan with their collaboration.

3. *Don't answer questions from the couple until ready.* In some cases, a question from a partner is designed to show how the other person is wrong, sick, or crazy. Questions need to be viewed with skepticism. The therapist needs to quickly assess whether the question has a hidden purpose or is designed to get the therapist to take sides. The therapist may respond to problematic questions by saying she/he doesn't know the answer yet or by deflecting the question, asking the questioner what she/he thinks and getting the partner to offer an opinion. Legitimate questions about the therapeutic process, such as how long, should be answered openly and honestly.

4. *Don't proceed until the problem(s) and goal(s) have been clarified.* Couples usually present with a number of different problems. In the initial session it is useful to get an overview and then come back to discuss the problem in some depth. Part of the process is deciding which problems to work on first, whether the presented problem is the real problem, and whether the partners desire the same resolution of the problem. The couple need to share a definition of the problem and the goals. Their ideas should be agreeable with the therapist and then interventions may be made.

5. *Don't discuss problems abstractly and nonconcretely.* Couples will sometimes begin therapy stating their difficulties in abstract, non-specific, nonbehavioral language (e.g., "We have communication problems"). This type of language does not lead to any understanding of the problem, particularly the sequence of behaviors involved in their reciprocal interactions. The therapist can quickly move from the abstract to the concrete by asking who, when, what, and how questions. By focusing the couple in this way, they will usually see what the therapist needs and alter their description of the problems.

6. *Don't discount problems, even small problems.* When partners come in together they are sometimes reluctant to discuss complaints openly, honestly, and with the intensity they actually feel about the problem. This tendency results in problems being understated or minimized. In some cases, the real problem is not brought up at all in the initial session because of the level of sensitivity, embar-

rassment, or shame associated with it. The therapist must listen with a "third ear" to what is being presented and as the relationship develops go back to those problems which may fall into this category. Problems that are often understated include alcohol and drug abuse, spouse abuse, and sexual difficulties.

In addition, the therapist could inadvertently fall into collusion with one partner by agreeing that the other partner's problem is not that distressing. For example, a wife may complain that her husband is not attentive enough. The husband may then discount her statement by giving numerous examples of being attentive. If the therapist summarily dismisses her complaint then she or he has colluded with the husband. In order to effectively join, the therapist must take each partner seriously.

7. *Don't allow differences to escalate.* Couples come to treatment when they are unable to resolve their differences. In all probability they have struggled over these differences for some time and with some intensity at home. During the assessment phase, the therapist does not want to escalate these differences. She or he wants to understand them. When the level of emotional intensity begins to escalate, the therapist can ask cognitively oriented questions (e.g., who, where, what, how) or shift to another topic, stating that it is clear the partners are very much at odds on the issue at hand and that it will be discussed later.

8. *Don't assume the partners in the couple will perceive the problem in the same way.* The reason the couple is coming to treatment is because they see things differently. The therapist should communicate this idea to the couple and not push for a similarity of perception. At this stage, it is useful to normalize differences, stating that it will take time to work through the problem. When the therapist communicates this attitude she/he is giving them permission to express their differences.

9. *Don't unbalance the system.* This guideline has two meanings. The first was discussed above in terms of not intervening until the therapist understands the problem(s), goal(s), and consequences of change. The second meaning deals with siding with one partner or accepting one partner's definition of the problem over the other's. Although it may be useful to conduct separate interviews during the evaluation phase, one of the greatest risks is that of appearing

to or actually siding with one partner. Each partner may be very convincing about the pathology in the other. The therapist should reserve judgment, stay neutral, and keep a systemic perspective unless all the data suggest otherwise.

10. *Don't make premature interpretations.* One of the fundamental techniques in psychotherapy is interpretation. In individual therapy, early and/or premature interpretations are often forgiven, overlooked, or constructively challenged. When an interpretation is made about one partner in the context of a couples session, the therapist may be seen as blaming or siding with one partner against the other. It is best to contain interpretations until enough information has been gathered to feel confident of its validity—and *only* after the joining process has been completed. The safest interpretations early in the treatment process are systemic (e.g., the two of you . . .) or bilateral (e.g., when one of you does _____, the other of you does _____).

11. *Don't get hooked in the past.* When couples begin treatment, it is easy for them to begin rehashing the past all over again. The therapist may see the 50th or 100th replay of an argument. The therapist's task is to enable the couple to talk about the past and how the past is currently affecting them, not to allow the couple to regress. The therapist may need to intervene actively and directly in cutting off this type of cycle. Questions designed to unravel the argument, get at individual meanings, and understand current feelings are helpful.

12. *Don't get hooked on the partner's theories or explanations.* It is useful to ask, if the partners don't volunteer, how they each explain the problem. One way to keep their theories from getting put forth as the truth is to ask simply, "What is your theory about the problem?" The question communicates that whatever answer is given is not going to be given the status of absolute truth. This information is useful in beginning to reframe or to redefine the problem. If the therapist's reframe is too incongruent with that of the couple, it will be rejected. Incorporating aspects of the couple's frame is more likely to meet with acceptance by the couple.

13. *Don't allow the couple to tell stories.* Some couples believe they have to tell stories in order to exemplify their problem. The stories may recount every detail and require a great deal of time to fully

tell. Allowing couples to tell stories is not a productive use of time. The therapist should attempt to get to the point that is being made by taking charge of the session. Otherwise, the therapist may be waiting 30 minutes while the full rendition is given. The therapist can begin by asking focused questions in order to obtain information that is clinically useful.

14. *Don't allow emotion to take charge of the session.* One or both partners may become emotionally distressed to the point of ruling the session. The therapist's task is to manage affect. In later sessions, the therapist may want to intensify and escalate affect. However, in order for the couple to feel safe and secure with the therapist early on, they must know the therapist is not frightened by their emotions and is able to keep them under control. In some relationships one partner is controlled by the emotions of the other. If the therapist allows this process to be repeated, the controlled partner will not see how the therapist can be helpful. Techniques to control affect are discussed later in this book in the chapter on Feelings.

15. *Don't allow the couple to take charge of the session.* One of the most difficult tasks for the beginning couples therapist, and for any therapist at the beginning of treatment, is how to take charge of what happens in the session. The therapist does not want to appear rigid or controlling, yet some partners/couples can be very controlling. In order to deal with these situations, the therapist can stick to the evaluation procedures outlined in this chapter in a businesslike fashion. Of course, if the couple are in crisis, the evaluation procedures are put on hold while the therapist takes charge of dealing with the crisis situation.

CASE FORMULATION

The case formulation proposed here is comprehensive. It requires the therapist to have a general and broad understanding of personality theory, psychotherapy, psychodiagnosis, and the major approaches to marital/family therapy. This approach to case formulation has been used in the training program at the Marriage Council of Philadelphia since 1985. The postdegree students in our program find it to be challenging and time consuming, as well as providing them with more insight than any other method they have employed. To develop the formulation, we use a form that our trainees must complete prior to supervision and initiating treatment. The remainder of this chapter will be devoted to reviewing this form item by item. Each section or question is numbered. These numbers will serve as reference points for the item-by-item description.

Item Descriptions

The first section of the form is general background information such as age, occupations, who else lives in the home besides nuclear family, and so on. It is also useful to know by whom and why the couple was referred. Permission should be obtained to talk with the referring therapist, often the therapist of one partner. The reason they were referred or referred themselves is very useful. Of all the reasons they might have for coming to treatment, most important is what was the precipitating event that motivated them at this particular time. Unless this question is asked, the therapist may not be told this critical event.

Item 1 deals with the therapist's initial impressions and reactions. It is the therapist's first and intuitive response to the couple. Clearly, this item is impressionistic and idiosyncratic. It consists of intuitions about the couple, strong emotional reactions observed and felt, and projections (countertransference) the therapist may experience. This item helps the clinician better understand the context in which the case is being formulated. For example, if the major initial reaction is one of extreme tension, fear, and suspicion in the couple, then all the data about the couple are filtered through this emotional environment. If the couple are open and relaxed and both partners take some responsibility for the problem, the therapist may believe what is being said is open, honest, and direct. The degree of probing and listening with a "third ear" would be needed less.

Item 2 has to do with obtaining a picture of the presenting problem(s). The therapist needs to get a clear and complete picture of all the problems. Each partner is permitted to express his/her perception of the problem. After each one has a turn, they may be asked to comment on the other person's perception of the problem. An essential part of asking about the presenting problem(s) is to get a sense of the problem from an interactional or circular perspective. The therapist is always searching for the contribution the other person makes to the problem. By exploring the sequence of behaviors through a complete cycle, the therapist may begin to discover the role of the other partner. What appears to be a problem in only one partner is actually part of an interlocking system of behavior.

CASE FORMULATION FORM

FAMILY NAME: _____ DATE OF 1ST INTERVIEW: _____

Partner's Name: _____ Age: ____ Occupation: _____

Partner's Name: _____ Age: ____ Occupation: _____

Children & Other Family in home:

_____   _____   _____

_____   _____

ETHNIC GROUP: _____ YRS. MARRIED/IN RELATIONSHIP: _____

REFERRED BY: _____ REASON FOR REFERRAL: _____

1. Initial Impressions and Reactions:

2. Presenting Problem(s)—Give a concrete description, including the who, where, what, how. What is each member's view of the problem? How is the problem maintained in the system?

3. History of the Problem—Abbreviated form of No. 2, above:

4. Solutions Attempted—(including previous therapy):

5. Changes Sought by Client(s):

6. Recent Significant Changes—Stressors & Life Cycle Changes (new job, move, death, divorce, child leaving home, etc.):

INTERSYSTEM ASSESSMENT

7. Individual System(s)—Intrapsychic components, i.e., cognitive distortions and irrational thinking, defense mechanisms (denial, projection), definitions, predictions, interpretations. Also include DSM-III-R diagnosis on Axis I, II, and III:

8. Interactional System—e.g., emotional contracts, styles of communication, patterns of dyadic interaction, linear attributional strategies (debilitation, justification, vilification, rationalization, conflict-resolution skills):

9. Intergenerational System—e.g., anniversary reactions, scripts, boundaries, cutoffs, triangles, closeness-distance issues:

TREATMENT PLAN

10. Hypothesis Regarding the Client(s):

11. Treatment Plan & Strategies: (Individual, Interactional, Intergenerational)

PROBLEMS	CHANGE STRATEGIES
1.	1.
2.	2.
3.	3.

12. Prognosis & Expected Length of Therapy: (Provisional)

13. What are your strengths and weaknesses in dealing with this client system?

Item 3 asks about the history of the problem(s). Once the current problem(s) is understood, it is useful to go back in time to find out whether the pattern has been the same or different. In some cases, the therapist may see the same pattern with reversals in roles. The problem(s) may predate the current relationship, having been present in all intimate relationships. If the problem has a beginning in time that can be identified, it is useful to know what precipitated it. Perhaps the problem began the day after marriage, after the discovery of an affair, or with the birth of a child.

Item 4 is aimed at getting some information about the solutions the couple have tried in order to solve the problem. In some cases the couple will have a history of therapy that was unsuccessful. The current therapist will want to know how or whether their previous therapy ended. Some couples jump from therapist to therapist prematurely with no therapist ever given a chance to help. Knowing what happened in the previous therapy lets the present therapist in on the problems discussed earlier and the efforts made to solve those problems. Because the previous therapy may have been unsuccessful or incomplete, the present therapist wants to avoid the mistakes made earlier.

Item 5 gives the therapist the opportunity to find out the couple's goals. After the couple have described their problem(s) and it is clear to the therapist what the problem is, the therapist should not make any assumptions about what kinds of changes are desired. Each partner should be asked what they want changed. The therapist must seek to help the couple jointly agree on the changes they want and collaboratively decide on the order in which the work shall be done.

Item 6 recognizes the importance of stressful events in precipitating and/or creating problems. The therapist may simply ask what changes and stresses have occurred during the last two years, especially the last six months. Many couples will not connect the level of change/stress in their lives to their problems. The number of changes in some couples is truly remarkable, and they should be helped to understand the consequences of these events.

The first six items of the case formulation are data-based. Subjective and objective information are gathered. The therapist sticks close to the data without drawing many inferences. Items 7, 8, and 9 are more inferential. The data are now being organized according to different levels and theoretical systems.

Item 7 may strike the couples therapist as odd within the context of a systemic approach. Marital and family therapy started as a reaction against individual psychopathology and therapy. For many years individual concepts have been viewed as antithetical to systems thinking. Yet, couples are composed of individuals. Each individual has his or her own set of dynamics and pathology. To deny this fact for the sake of taking a pure systems perspective would be unnecessarily dogmatic and also limiting. Consequently, we suggest an assessment of each individual's intrapsychic dynamics. This includes, but is not limited to, the individual's use of defense mechanisms, cognitive distortions, and the concepts of definitions, predictions, and interpretations mentioned earlier in the introductory chapter.

The issue of individual psychopathology requires the therapist to consider the interlocking nature of psychopathology. In our companion text, Goldberg (1987) discussed how to view individual pathology from a systems perspective. An assumption in systems theories is that partners are ✶ equally healthy or unhealthy and that the severity of individual pathology is often quite similar. That notwithstanding, an area which has been neglected in diagnosis with couples is that of personality disorders. We see numerous cases in which partners present with personality disorders or traits of personality disorders. Some common combinations are the narcissistic/dependent or inadequate, obsessive-compulsive/histrionic and borderline, and aggressive/dependent types. Millon (1981) has written extensively about these personality types in his book entitled *Disorders of Personality.*

Individual diagnoses help the therapist understand and treat the interlocking part of the pathology. The couple may also need concurrent individual therapy which is coordinated with the couples therapist. Obviously, some individual pathologies require attention prior to the onset of couples therapy. Severe psychopathology is a clear contraindication for couples therapy. Cases involving psychosis, severe depression, suicide, and drugs/alcohol abuse all require individual attention first. In general, individual diagnosis should not be shared with the couple as it may be used by one partner to project more blame or craziness onto the other.

Item 8 is the one most directly concerned with the couple's functioning. This item involves assessing the interactional problems of the couple in accord with any number of marital therapies and concepts. Some of the common concepts in this category deal with deficits in communication and conflict-resolution skills, emotional contracts, interlocking cognitive distortions, and inappropriate and blocked emotions. Special emphasis should be given to understanding how the couple uses attributional strategies which are designed to externalize personal responsibility and blame the other partner for the marital problems. In couples, the spouse bearing the symptom (e.g., depression) may simply blame the other partner for the dysfunctional mood. The linear attributional tactics seen in couples is, however, more varied than simple projection.

Four methods of destructive linear attribution have been identified by Strong and Claiborn (1982):

1) *Justification* is the practice of assigning the negative or harmful effects of one's behavior onto external causes (e.g., "I cannot help the way I act because of my crazy family");

2) *Rationalization* is the practice of denying that one's internally controlled behavior was intended to be harmful (e.g., "I just did it [it is being overcontrolling] to help you");

3) *Debilitation* involves assigning hurtful behavior to causes inside but beyond one's control (e.g., "I cannot help it, when you do that, I go off. . . . You should know that and stop what you are doing"); and

4) *Vilification,* in which the other person is made a villain by attributing negative intent to him or her. Consequently, the partner's behavior is justified as a response to hurtful behavior (e.g., "You just have to put me down in front of your family so you can feel superior").

The therapist may note whether these tactics are being used and then work toward eliminating them.

Item 9 is concerned with how family-of-origin issues may play a role in the marital dynamics. Patterns learned in the family of origin tend to be repeated in later relationships. It is beyond the scope of this section to describe all of these patterns. Readers should be familiar with the major concepts of Bowen's theory (see Kerr, 1981) and the genogram assessments in *Genograms in Family Assessment* by McGoldrick and Gerson (1985). In addition to the concepts found in these books, there are questions or issues that deserve mention. They are:

1. What were the roles you observed in your parents' marriage?
2. What did your parents appear to expect from each other?
3. What did you learn about being a husband/wife?

4. How much closeness/distance did you see in your parents?
5. How did your parents handle their anger and conflict?
6. Did your parents show their affection/intimacy openly?
7. How did your parents order their priorities among self, marriage, children, and work?
8. What emotions were encouraged, allowed, not allowed, denied, said to be bad?
9. Were there any traumas in your parents' marriage such as affairs, incest, unresolved grief, or psychological and medical problems?
10. What did you learn about intimacy from your parents?

In cases where the couple are also presenting with a sexual problem, another series of questions is useful. Larry Hof (in Weeks & Hof, 1987) and Weeks (1987) have found that some sexual problems are rooted in family history. Hof has developed a set of questions to help obtain information pertinent in these cases. These questions are listed below:

The Sexual Genogram Process

1. Introduction—Explain and discuss the role of early learning and intergenerational processes in the development of individual, couple, and family systems. "Life Scripts," "Family Scripts," "Family Loyalties."
2. Creation and Exploration of a Genogram—Graphic depictions of three or four generations of each partner's family (if couple-oriented) or of the individual's family, emphasizing facts, feelings, alliances, boundaries, coalitions, closeness, distance, emotional cutoffs, conflicts, connectedness, and so on.
3. Creation and Exploration of a Sexual Genogram—Reconsideration of the multigenerational system with a specific focus on pointed questions relating to sexuality and intimacy.

   a) What are the overt/covert messages in this family regarding sexuality/intimacy? Regarding masculinity/femininity?
   b) Who said/did what? Who was conspicuously silent/absent in the area of sexuality/intimacy?
   c) Who was the most open sexually? Intimately? In what ways?
   d) How was sexuality/intimacy encouraged? Discouraged? Controlled? Within a generation? Between generations?

   e)   What questions have you had regarding sexuality/intimacy in your "family tree" that you have been reluctant to ask? Who might have the answers? How could you discover the answers?

   f)   What were the "secrets" in your family regarding sexuality/intimacy (e.g., incest, unwanted pregnancies, extramarital affairs, etc.)?

   g)   What do the other "players on the stage" have to say regarding the above questions? How did these issues, events, and experiences impact upon him/her? Within a generation? Between generations? With whom have you talked about this? With whom would you like to talk about this? How could you do it?

   h)   How does your partner perceive your family tree/genogram regarding the aforementioned issues? How do you perceive his/hers?

   i)   How would you change this genogram (including Who and What) to meet what you wish would have occurred regarding messages and experiences of sexuality/intimacy?

  4. Exploration and Discussion of Genogram Material/Issues with Extended Family Members—Review of the total process and integration within the treatment plan for sexual dysfunction.

Genogram assessment may be done early on, later on, or scattered throughout the assessment and treatment phase. The use of these questions depends on the extent to which the problem appears to have an historical versus current basis.

Item 10 consists of the therapist's hypotheses based on all the data. To begin treatment involves making some basic hypotheses about the nature and causes of the problem. The major hypotheses are listed in this section. For example, the therapist might hypothesize that the basic problem is one of closeness and distance based on the husband's experience of a rejecting mother and the wife's experience of incest with her stepfather.

Hypotheses are "tested" as treatment proceeds. If the hypotheses produce the desired outcome for everyone, the hypotheses are probably valid. If not, it might be time to reconsider the hypotheses.

Item 11 is the treatment plan and change strategies. Marital therapists have not stressed this aspect of treatment enough in their work. For each category of assessment, a treatment goal and strategy may be formulated.

For an individual with severe depression, a referral to a psychiatrist would be an appropriate strategy. In the same case, the denial of depression in the other partner might require a reframe of the depression so that the "unaffected" partner sees his/her role in the depression in the system. There also might be an intergenerational pattern of depressed women in the family requiring some family-of-origin work, accompanied by sessions involving mother and grandmother. The treatment plan can involve any combination of techniques, approaches, or strategies. The plan needs to be developed with an awareness of which changes to make first, the couple's readiness for work in different problem areas, and how to build sequentially on successes.

Item 12 is the therapist's prognosis and estimated length of treatment. It is useful for the therapist to be realistic about the outcome of therapy and to share the most probable outcome with the couple following the evaluation phase. In so doing, the couple will not be operating on their assumptions about what to expect. Couples often ask about the length of treatment. Being realistic means starting with a valid contract. If a couple will need at least six months and they are unwilling to go more than six weeks, there is no basis for a working relationship. When the therapist has followed the procedures outlined above she or he can explain which problems will be treated, how, with what probable success, and for roughly how long. The couple can then make an informed decision about continuing treatment.

Item 13 is designed to help the therapist recognize the strengths he or she brings to the case and potential countertransference issues. One therapist may find he or she has significant experience in working with conflict in couples, while another is intimidated by anger in men because of personal history. The therapist who experiences a countertransference reaction from the outset should seek supervision and/or therapy to resolve this problem. If the therapist is unwilling to be responsible for the countertransference reaction, the case should be referred. Treating a case when there is a countertransference reaction is at best likely to be unsuccessful and at worst damaging to the couple.

The 13 items covered in this approach to case formulation are by no means exhaustive or unique. It is the combination of items that makes this approach stand out as more comprehensive than others. As the marital therapist becomes more knowledgeable and practiced in this approach, this series of questions will become second nature. To reach this point will require time and persistence.

CONCLUSION

The purpose of this chapter was to discuss two topics. First guidelines for conducting the first few sessions were offered. These guidelines are designed to help the couple therapist avoid some of the more common difficulties in getting started with the couple. The guidelines are just what we call them; they are not hard and fast rules that must be adhered to strictly. The therapist should use her or his own judgment in deciding when these guides do not fit. Following the assessment/engagement phase of treatment, it is much less important to follow these guides. In fact, they may be counterindicated in some circumstances. For example, the therapist may later want to unbalance the system by temporarily taking sides. This procedure would be done for therapeutic, not diagnostic reasons.

The second issue covered in this chapter was assessment. Assessment and treatment are usually blended in doing couples work. The difference is in the emphasis paid to one or the other. The approach described reveals a procedure for collecting a tremendous amount of information in a systematic way. Some of the information may be collected much later in treatment as the need arises and as the need to further develop the treatment plan emerges. During the assessment phase, at least enough information should be collected to permit the development of our initial case formulation. The case formulation is the basic road map that enables the therapist to begin the course of treatment.

Chapter 2

Orienting Couples to Therapy

A couple's myths about the nature of marital therapy and the unrealistic expectations concerning the therapist's role can get the therapeutic process off to a difficult start. One of the tasks of the therapist is to teach couples about these realistic and unrealistic expectations. Appropriate expectations can set a positive tone for the entire therapy and for the couple's relationship with the therapist.

Important tasks for the marital therapist are: (1) to inquire about general couple expectations for the therapy and to educate where necessary; (2) to teach couples about specific boundary issues pertaining to length of appointments, lateness, use of telephone, fees, missed appointments, and so on; (3) to discuss general expectations of the therapeutic process, for example, instructing a couple on how to take responsibility for a session; discussing who speaks to whom and the importance of balance; and advising the couple not to quote the therapist in a negative fashion during arguments or discussions at home. When these issues are clear, the clients can benefit more from the therapy hour. This chapter will cover each of these tasks.

UNREALISTIC EXPECTATIONS

The therapist needs to inquire about the reasons a couple has initiated therapy and to educate them about any misconceptions. The following misconceptions are often held by clients during a beginning session.

"We are going to the therapist so that she or he will tell us what to do."

In most cases, instructing clients how to behave or what to do next is not a therapist's role. A systemically trained therapist is not seeking regressive behavior or dependency from a couple. Instead, encouraging active couple participation and insight into areas of difficulty, as well as facilitating behavioral change are desired. A therapist could share several images depicting the relationship of client and therapist, such as, *a guide* to help the couple step out of confusion, *a teacher* with whom to explore relationships, *a confronter* of possible cognitive distortions or dysfunctional behavior, *a referee* to maintain some balance and fairness in the couple's communication, or *a friend* to walk with during times of stress and depression. Many images and roles are applicable for the marital therapist. There are also some roles that are generally not appropriate. In most cases a marital therapist should not be: a mother or father leading dependent children, an all-knowing person who does not respect the intelligence of the client, or the sole interpreter of truth and the meaning of life. The therapist should not claim to possess a monopoly on what is right or wrong for a client or be a friend who relates to couples outside of the therapeutic setting.

"I'm afraid we will be doing all of the talking and the marital therapist won't be saying anything at all."

Systemic therapists are most often active and directive, not passive. If clients come to therapy feeling angry about certain issues and an argument ensues, they are probably reenacting a communication pattern repeated many times in private. Such a couple may be seeking therapy in the hope of breaking this repetitive communication and exploring feelings of discouragement or rejection. The passivity of the marital therapist can and probably will lead to more couple conflict and feelings of despair.

Lack of interaction between the therapist and clients is one of the primary reasons couples leave therapy. Often, a couple is searching for someone who will institute some control, structure, fairness, boundaries, and the confidence that their relationship could be different in the future. To accomplish these goals the therapist's primary tools are sharing insight, structuring behaviors, changing process, assigning homework, and creatively using his or her personality. The marital therapist needs to demonstrate an active stance during the initial stages of therapy to raise the hope that interactions could be less dysfunctional and more nurturing and healing in the future.

"I did not think that a marital and family therapist would work with an individual."

Systemic issues can be approached in the context of an entire family, a couple or friendship, or an individual's relationships. In the systemic framework, change in an individual's behavior can affect a couple or a family as directly as change in the couple or family can affect an individual.

One mistake that many therapists make is to turn away an individual coming to work on his or her marriage when one partner refuses to participate. A partner who can understand how different patterns have developed within a relationship can begin to realize the part she or he might play in those patterns—and eventually considerably affect the quality of a marriage. In other words, the partner can begin to understand the circular nature of his or her relationship, that is, how the communications of one partner elicit a response in the other partner and vice versa. On the other hand, if the partner who comes to therapy insists on spending the therapeutic time projecting onto his or her absent partner all of the responsibility for the problems in the relationship, the therapy will probably not be very fruitful. These clients see the problems in linear terms by blaming their partners for the conflict in spite of what the therapist points out about how such a view is counterproductive.

A frequent mistake a therapist can make is to alienate the presenting individual client by having him or her "beg" the absent partner to come into therapy. The more a reluctant or outright resistant spouse is pressed, the more power the individual may lose in the marital relationship. This is because the most power in a relationship is held by the person with the least investment in whatever is being pursued. If the reluctant partner finally agrees to come in, his or her attitude is often expressed thusly, "How can I help you change, because I don't have a problem?" Such placing of responsibility onto the partner, and lack of desire to be in therapy, will probably undermine the process.

"The success of the therapeutic process is based on the skill of the therapist."

The insight and skill of the therapist are certainly key components to the success of the therapy. However, a seasoned therapist will realize and accept his or her limitations when clients are highly resistant to working productively on the relationship. A client needs to be taught that responsibility for movement in therapy depends on every participant. The inexperienced therapist who is overly anxious or insecure can assume too much responsibility for change. For example, he or she could lecture or be more invested in client growth than the couple. In so doing, she or he can inadvertently teach the client not to be self-responsible. Getting both partners to accept responsibility for the problem is a goal of the systemic therapist. Then, when change occurs, the clients can attribute the change to themselves and not to the therapist. The therapist who claims responsibility for client growth and movement infantilizes the couple and diminishes the effectiveness of therapy.

"A male or female therapist will be more sensitive to my needs."

A competent therapist of either gender will be able to maintain balance and be just to both partners. Maintaining balance involves confronting, sharing empathy, and talking to each partner in an equal and fair manner. (refer to Chapter 3) The therapist who continually ends up siding with one gender or the other is in need of personal therapy before continuing to practice marital therapy. Continual siding suggests transference or countertransference issues that the therapist may not have worked through from his or her experiences in the family of origin. Sometimes it is helpful for the therapist, especially if she or he senses one client is fearful of being sided against, to verbalize how every attempt will be made to keep a balanced perspective and to look at mutual responsibility. For instance, saying to a client, "Do you think that because I am male/female I may be more likely to side with one of you?" Direct questioning to a couple might calm anxieties about issues of fairness in terms of gender and make the clients aware that the therapist recognizes and understands such concerns. The therapist may also ask the couple to voice their concerns during conjoint therapy if they believe the therapist is siding on the basis of gender.

If the client maintains the bias that one gender will be more sensitive to specific issues, and is resistant to the therapy, referral should be offered. It is probably better client care and more productive for the therapeutic process to help the client begin therapy with a minimal amount of prejudice.

"Once the therapeutic process begins, it will never end."

Clients sometimes fear entering a therapeutic process without knowing how to leave. It is often helpful for the therapist to explain that this process is to help them, that it was their initiation that determined when they entered, and that they will determine how much each invests in the process and when they are ready to terminate. A therapist who needs a particular client for ego gratification or financial security should not be doing therapy. Such needs can override sound therapeutic judgment. Clients entering marital therapy can be taught that the duration of marital and family therapy averages anywhere from several sessions to several years. If members of a couple feel they have the power to determine the length and frequency of therapy, they are more likely to invest in the process. A therapist might say to a client, "I'm not sure how long the therapeutic process should last. In general, therapy continues until your goals are achieved. Many variables can contribute to that decision. First let's see if it is helpful, and if not, we can decide on other directions or I can refer you to another therapist."

GENERAL BOUNDARY ISSUES

Most couples come to therapy with some difficulty in establishing effective boundaries. Many couples are enmeshed or disengaged due in part to boundary problems in their respective families of origin. If the therapy and the therapeutic relationship between client and therapist does not model healthy boundaries (i.e., flexible rather than rigid or chaotic), the client's dysfunctional boundary problems can be reenacted in the therapist-client relationship and in the overall therapeutic process. The therapist needs to maintain appropriate boundaries in both the content and process of therapy. The following discussion will illustrate and explain five kinds of boundary issues.

Length of Sessions

Most therapists work on a 50-minute hour. Clients need to be told this limit directly and, if possible, to have their check written out before the session begins. The process of finding the checkbook, writing the check, figuring out the correct date, and recording the correct check number, while often talking to the therapist at the same time, is an awkward and cumbersome period of time. A client has the right to a full session and the therapist has the right to take a break before the next therapeutic hour begins.

The reasons a therapist might not boundary time appropriately are quite diverse and most often indicative of unresolved personal issues or insufficient structuring skills. Possibly, the therapist is taking too much responsibility for the movement or growth of the couple and believes that one more intervention will make the difference. One of the worst effects of not placing boundaries on the length of a session is that client resistance to dealing with significant material sooner in the therapeutic hour is reinforced. A client who knows that the therapist is going to start and stop on time is much more likely to be prompt and invest in substantive material early in the session. It is a myth to think that because some movement and insight were achieved in one hour, twice as much can be accomplished in two hours.

Lateness

In general, if a couple is late for a session and the therapist accommodates by exceeding the allotted hour, they will be reinforced to not worry about being prompt. The therapist can unwittingly collude in a couple's resistance and manipulation by not setting limits. Lack of personal limit setting can result in a therapist feeling disrespected and abused. A therapist should explain to the couple that if they are late, the time cannot be made up; however, if the therapist is late, the full 50-minute session will take place.

In marital therapy, one protection against triangulation of the therapist is to not visit with the one partner of a couple who comes on time. A therapy session begins when both partners arrive. Waiting for both partners to be present before therapy begins is a rule that should be explained to the clients.

Missed Appointments

In the first session, it is helpful to lay down the ground rules concerning missed appointments. If the therapist makes a mistake and schedules two clients at the same time—in our experience, a rare occurrence—it is important that he or she makes up the session for the couple who is turned away and does not charge them for that session. The client has made the trip to therapy twice and has been seen only once. If the client misses an appointment, especially more than once, the therapist in most cases should charge the client and set up another time to meet. The therapist who communicates clearly to a couple or family that at least 24 hours notice is needed for a cancellation, or the therapy hour will be charged, demonstrates appropriate boundaries and self-respect. Therapists who do not set up these kind of parameters will find themselves feeling abused by the whims of clients who are too tired to come to therapy or who found, due to resistance, something more "fun" to do.

Phones, Knocking, and General Disturbance

Many couples come to therapy because they have been unable to establish effective boundaries regarding their children, parents, work or personal lives to allow for strengthening and protecting their marital relationship. The therapy must model appropriate boundaries which are needed for a couple to develop definition, security, and stability. The therapist can inform clients that in general during a session they will not be disturbed. The therapist will not answer the phone, go to the door, or do anything that would take away from the primary therapist-client relationship. In turn, the therapist does not want to have a client knock on a closed door, but to wait in the appointed waiting area.

With some possible exceptions, a client should be taught to honor the boundaries of the therapist and not call him or her at home. Clients with few boundaries can intrude upon the therapist's private time and undermine the therapy by having private conversations which exclude one partner. An exception might be a therapist giving his or her telephone number, and permission to use it, as a demonstration of caring and concern. Sometimes it is easier for a therapist to request that a client call during certain hours to change appointments or express concerns that can't wait until the next session, instead of playing telephone tag. In general, the more a therapist feels that a client will honor the boundaries and respect the time of the therapist, the freer the therapist might be to give out his or her telephone number. If the therapist misjudges and ends up getting interrupted unnecessarily, she or he needs to be able to effectively boundary the client from use of the phone and further intrusion.

Payment

Therapists who are confident about the services they provide feel appropriately entitled to directly receive payment for their services at the conclusion of each session. Therapists who do not receive payment from a client do the therapeutic process an injustice. A client who pays a receptionist might devalue the therapy or therapist. Couples who do not pay may resist working, prolong the length of therapy, or in a passive-aggressive manner set up the therapist to become angry. Furthermore, a therapist who does not insist on payment can establish client indebtedness and a subsequent imbalance of power. When a client feels that he or she owes a therapist, the dynamics of guilt and obligation can be manipulated. For instance, a couple may not leave therapy when they feel it is appropriate because the therapist has been so generous with his or her time, or a therapist might manipulate a couple to stay in therapy by sharing feelings of self-sacrifice. A practical matter is that when a therapist is not paid directly, unpaid client bills are almost always higher.

If the therapist charges on a sliding scale, the negotiation of a fee for service gives the therapist a great deal of information about the client, and the client gains insight into the therapist. The therapist can learn how resistant a couple might be if comments by the couple in the negotiation suggest that therapy might not be a priority. Early patterns of manipulation might appear at this time when a couple hedges on the actual amount of their income. Cries of poverty, combined with planned vacations on a later date, can create feelings in the therapist of being used.

Conversely, a couple who negotiates in good faith for a lower fee or agree to the fee presented by the therapist can communicate a respect for the therapy, personal motivation, and the value of the therapist's time. A client learns a great deal about the therapist who lowers every fee and doesn't insist on payment. Perhaps the therapist does not value his or her time or have a high regard for his or her competence. The way a therapist negotiates fees, the degree of flexibilty, the tone of voice, and the level of anxiety can raise hope and respect or, conversely, erode confidence in the therapist.

In general, negotiation of the fee is a good way for the therapist to learn about client investment, resistance, control needs, and assertiveness, while the client can learn about a therapist's professional identity and confidence. At best, the dynamics surrounding the setting of fees and timely payment teach effective boundaries and self-respect. At worst, it becomes a dysfunctional aspect of the client-therapist relationship.

GENERAL EXPECTATIONS OF THE THERAPEUTIC PROCESS

Issues of Personal Responsibility

"Tell me what to do." Many couples make this statement directly, while others indirectly attempt to get the therapist to claim or to take responsibility for change. The therapist who takes responsibility for the content and emotional energy of a session might find himself or herself working very hard, often exhausted at the end of the session. Furthermore, a client who does not accept enough responsibility can have the luxury of sitting back in a resistance mode, wondering why the therapist is not more effective.

Enabling the Client to Begin the Session

In between sessions, the couple should be working on their relationship and planning to bring to therapy communication difficulties, insights, and issues that stymie or confuse them. If clients know that their session will begin with a directive or structure chosen or imposed by the therapist, they will most likely be passive and defer responsibility to the therapist. If the direction and content of the therapeutic hour is left to the initiation of the clients, they are more likely to have talked and processed material between sessions and will arrive at therapy with issues and concerns on which to focus. A therapist who gives responsibility to clients will begin a session with silence or with an open-ended question. Open-ended questions do not guide the content of the answer or the direction of the session. Examples are:

- Where would you like to begin?
- What should we talk about today?
- How would you like to use this time?

Therapists mistakenly believe they are giving responsibility to the clients when they ask closed-ended questions, but in fact they are controlling the content and process almost entirely. Examples are:

- Have you been feeling angry? (A client then talks about feeling angry instead of anything else.)
- Did you do your homework last week? (Then the client does not begin with the feeling or idea that he or she wanted or intended to share or discuss.)
- Would you like to begin with what you said last week? (Clearly the therapist is setting the agenda. This information can be requested at a later time in the session, but hopefully not at the expense of the couple's agenda.)

Another type of interaction that results in transferring responsibility from the clients to the therapist is when clients' passivity is demonstrated in the "question and answer game." An example of this kind of very difficult interaction is given below:

Therapist: How are you today?
Couple: Fine.
Therapist: What would you like to talk about?
Couple: We aren't sure.
Therapist: How about discussing the intimacy in the relationship?
Couple: What about?

This type of question and answer sequence can be endless. In such a process, the client takes little responsibility for exploration into personal issues or difficulties, and the therapist continually tries to guess what would be meaningful content. A therapist will know that this dynamic is occurring when he or she is spending all of his or her mental energy in the session trying to figure out the next question. By worrying about how to frame the next question during an interactive process, the therapist will be distracted and will not be able to listen effectively to the clients. When a couple take responsibility for the content and process of a therapeutic hour, a therapist can monitor and guide instead of remaining responsible for the content of the interaction.

Another difficulty with a question and answer process, when used during initial sessions, is that of setting a standard and/or expectation for the couple about what the therapy is going to entail. Once this mental set has been established, it is difficult for couples to make the shift from the therapist asking questions to taking responsibility for the content of the session. An intake should not only include therapist inquiry, but also give to the couple a sense of their central role through their interaction and exploration. Couples begin to learn that they have some responsibility from the very first session.

A therapist might encourage client responsibility and investment by saying something like, "I could ask you many questions that I may deem important, but I would rather focus on your ideas, perceptions, and questions and have you talk about them together. I won't be silent for long and will ask for clarification and insight into your understanding of the strengths and weaknesses of your relationship." The skill in this process is to explore the relationship with the couple through the themes and emotions that may surface as the clients take responsibility for sharing the presenting problem(s).

This approach is in contrast to asking unrelated questions about the couple relationship and family of origin as if the therapist were reading off a list. For example, if a couple state that they feel the relationship has grown very distant, the therapist can orient the discussion about the relationship and the family of origin around the idea of distance. The history, feelings, origins, and behaviors of the couple can all be explored using distance as a theme. If a wife states that she feels very abandoned and the husband retorts that he feels smothered, the feelings of abandonment and smothering can be focused upon and explored as the therapist gets to know the couple through the concerns and feelings of the couple and not the unrelated packaged questions of the therapist. Using the themes and feelings presented by the clients places responsibility for the presentation of material with the clients and not on the questions of the therapist.

Facilitating Communication Between Spouses as Central to the Process of Marital Therapy

The marital therapist should create the expectation that the couple will come to therapy having talked at home and will be prepared to discuss significant issues both between themselves and with the therapist. To establish the above expectations, part of the initial session should include the couple spending time talking to each other while the therapist observes. This dialogue helps in the assessment of reciprocal patterns, which then can begin to be processed in the session.

The most natural way to introduce the idea that the therapist would like the couple to talk to each other is to redirect the conversation away from the therapist to between the partners. Most often each partner will be intent on sharing directly with the therapist her or his specific version of the difficulties. While it is important for the therapist to hear and respond to each individual to facilitate joining, ultimately it will be positive couple communication that will create some healing and reconciliation. With repeated therapist insistence on partner communication, the couple will soon realize that the therapist will not fill up therapeutic time with lectures and advice, but is far more interested in the couple's communication patterns in and out of therapy.

Confronting Blame and Judgment and Inspiring Self-responsibility

The most common presentation in therapy by each spouse is to place blame and responsibility for the marital difficulties on the other partner. As both are sure that the other is the primary cause of the difficulty, each attempts to align the therapist to his or her perception. As the marital therapist stays balanced and fair, she or he attempts to empower the clients by helping them to see their specific contributions and to begin the process of accepting responsibility. Clients have a great deal of power to change themselves and very minimal power to change their partners. Communication patterns are most often characterized by blaming. These patterns can be broken through the client's acceptance of individual responsibility and behavioral change.

Warning the Client Against Quoting the Therapist or Using the Therapist's Name at Home in a Destructive Manner

It is sometimes helpful to ask that the therapist's name not be used negatively in order to support one person's perception over the other in the couple's communication at home. "Dr._____ said . . ."—especially when attached to a misquoted or badly communicated "fact"—can create anger and dissatisfaction over the therapy. If the conversation gets heated enough, both partners might become angry with and attribute blame to the therapist. If clients do repeat information, feelings, or ideas about a session, they most often should communicate them as their own subjective experience. "I believe" instead of "the therapist said" will lead to a healthier communication without putting the therapist in the middle of every conversation.

The use of the therapist's name can be useful in specific couple interaction if each individual has a positive regard for the therapist and a desire to share sensitively and reflectively with his or her partner. "Dr. ____ said that we should be talking amongst ourselves, how about tonight?" is an example of a couple using the name of the therapist positively in order to strengthen their resolve and initiate more intimate comunication.

CONCLUSION

In summary, many couples come to therapy with apprehension, unrealistic expectations, and a lack of information about the roles and boundaries of client, therapist, and therapeutic process. Educating the client on some of the above mentioned issues—and making what might seem obvious to the therapist explicit to the couple—can prevent a great deal of misunderstanding and help the therapy begin in a healthier, more productive manner.

Chapter 3

Balanced Intervention

The concept of balance is central to systemic thought and the process of marital therapy. When the therapist thinks systemically, she or he believes that both partners of a marital dyad contribute to the difficulties they might be experiencing. The marital therapist who is balanced in approach asks both partners to be accountable, confronts both with relatively equal intensity, and finds ways to be supportive and nurturing to each person. In such an approach, the marital therapist does not align with one partner or form a coalition against the other, but consistently addresses the influence and contribution of both spouses. If the therapist loses balance, the therapy is often destructive to one or both marital partners. Judgment and fault can take the place of personal responsibility and the establishment of a climate of fairness and trust. The clients' perception that the therapist is not balanced or fair is one of the main reasons for early termination.

This chapter will discuss several techniques for a balanced approach to individual partners in dyadic therapy. These techniques involve the therapist joining with clients in a balanced way, educating couples about the importance of the therapist's balanced approach, and structuring therapy in a balanced way. Included will be considerations of the clients' understanding of balance, inclusive language, intensity and balance, and seating arrangement to promote balance. Understanding psychopharmacology and balance, determining therapeutic balance, and examining the potential for the loss of balance as a vital area for personal insight and growth will conclude the chapter.

JOINING WITH CLIENTS

It is most important to establish balance during the process of introducing oneself and getting to know a couple in the initial session.

New clients will be especially sensitive to the balancing skills and objectivity of the therapist. The following are some commonsense ideas for the therapist to use in order to join with the couple and establish a balanced approach.

1. Shake the hands of *both* husband and wife.
2. If small talk prevails for the opening minutes, make sure you are as invested in the conversation with the husband as with the wife, and vice versa.
3. When asking for the presenting problem, try not to allow one partner to monopolize the conversation for too long. While the verbosity of one spouse and the quiet of the other is "grist for the mill" in assessing marital dynamics, letting one person dominate in the opening session could create destructive alignments. To be fair, the therapist might have to stop a person in the middle of his or her discourse, or to look to the partner and simply ask for his or her perspective or response.
4. A first session would include the therapist seeking to understand the perceptions of both partners to let each know that what he or she has to say is important.
5. Opening attempts at assessment should be very balanced and fair in terms of responsibility; never confront only one partner. For example, "I can see how you elicit this from him and how you elicit this from her."

EDUCATING CLIENTS

It is often difficult for the therapist to approach a dyad in a balanced way. Many clients will attempt to persuade the therapist that his or her particular view of the marital relationship is correct (usually that the partner is at fault). In the initial stages of therapy, there is frequently a battle for the loyalty of the therapist. In addition, the couple often enter the therapeutic process already experiencing the advice and counsel of individually aligned friends and family members.

Educating clients about the importance of the therapist being balanced is crucial. When such education is done well, time that otherwise would have been spent justifying individual positions and perspectives is frequently saved. At the beginning or the end of the initial session, the marital therapist can make the following statements and discuss the following balance and process issues with the couple:

- I am going to work hard to understand both of your perspectives. Both of you are key to making effective change.
- I am going to try to be very balanced in my approach. What this means is that I assume that both of you have some responsibility for the problems and the solutions, and that each of your contributions to the problems will be addressed.
- I am going to try not to take sides. I can feel each of you trying to convince me of the rightness of your perspective, but if I do my job well, I will remain fairly neutral.
- If you feel unfairly sided against or judged by me, please let me know. It is not my intent, and I want to talk about it right away when you feel it happening.
- In order for the marriage to become more nurturing, both of you must begin to think more systemically. We will talk about this often, but briefly it means that behavior does not happen in a vacuum, and that the ways you are both treating each other are circular in nature—each of you influences the responses of the other. Each of you needs to take some responsibility for creating and continuing the circular and negative interactions.

The above are examples of how to educate clients about the systemic and balanced approach. When the education is explicit, trust can develop and the healing process will often proceed at a quicker pace.

OVERALL STRUCTURE OF THERAPY: WHO PARTICIPATES?

There are many views about who should participate in the therapeutic process. Many individual psychotherapists believe that in-depth work can be done only during the course of an individual session. Some marital and family therapists conceptualize therapy as needing to include every member of the family. Others believe couple work includes only partners. Whatever the perspective, several key considerations are important for the maintenance of a balanced approach.

1. If the therapist sees the wife for an individual session in the beginning of therapy, the husband should also be seen separately.

2. If individual sessions are deemed necessary to break up emotional blocks or enmeshment, the number of individual sessions should be approximately equal for the partners.
3. If one individual appears for a session when both partners were supposed to be present, it is a judgment call on whether the therapist should see the individual client. If the individual client is seen, the next session might be an individual one for the other partner in order to maintain balance.
4. Often individual therapy will evolve into couples therapy. If the individual has been in therapy for a long time, it is problematic whether the current therapist ought to do the conjoint work. In many cases this can be counterproductive because loyalties, real or perceived, have been established. If it is decided that the same therapist should do both the individual and the conjoint therapy, several techniques to balance loyalties and alignments are important. The longstanding individual client must be educated about what feelings he or she might anticipate when the partner is included in the therapy. The education might include saying the following:

> When your partner is included in the therapy, you might very well experience some feelings of loss or of being judged by me. I will attempt to be very balanced in my approach and will try to understand your spouse's perspectives as well as yours. Because you have felt my loyalty, you might feel this as a betrayal. If you do, let's process this in the conjoint session.

In terms of structuring the session, an effective approach to try to establish a sense of balance might be to see the partner who is joining the therapy in several individual sessions. During this time, the therapist can listen to his or her perspectives and show some empathy for his or her position. It may be helpful to make clear that the transition from individual therapy to couples therapy is provisional, and if it is not helpful, other alternatives will be sought. What is crucial to process directly with the spouse entering therapy is the following:

> I am concerned that you will feel that my approach to both of you is fair. There is a danger in what we are about to do in that you might feel aligned or "ganged up" against. I am going to try to be

very balanced. However, if you feel otherwise, please let me know immediately.

CLIENT UNDERSTANDING OF BALANCE

A primary fear of the individual spouse in a couples session is that the therapist will blame, focus upon, or confront one partner more intensely than the other. In a balanced approach, the timing of confrontation is very important. When the marital therapist decides to confront one individual at a time, it is crucial that the partner who is first being confronted or asked probing questions about his or her complicity in a certain dynamic trusts that the partner will also be confronted in a similar manner. To establish balance and build trust, the marital therapist can make statements such as:

- "I am going to ask you both the same question."
- "I will want you both to take a turn."
- "What is your responsibility? And, in a minute, what is yours?"
- "I will ask you both to respond to what your understanding is."

The importance of timing is that the spouse who is first confronted needs to understand prior to making a response that his or her partner will be asked a question or comment of similar intensity next. Consider the following interaction in which the promise of a balanced approach is not adequately established prior to the confrontation.

Therapist to Wife: Can you see what you were doing in that last interaction?
Wife: I was just trying to express myself.
Therapist: You were expressing yourself in a very judgmental way.
Wife: But he never listens to me and just walks away.
Therapist: Your judgment pushes your husband away.

Note what each of the three parties present in the therapy session could be thinking while this particular dynamic is taking place. The wife might be feeling unfairly judged and confronted by the therapist. She cannot understand why the therapist does not confront her husband. Consequently, she spends most of the time—in response to the therapist's intervention—being defensive and trying to convince the therapist of the husband's role. The therapist might be thinking in a systemic manner, but is not functioning in one. It may be in his or her mind to confront the husband next; however, she or he has not communicated this fact to the wife and ends up fielding her defensiveness. The husband is thinking that the therapist understands how his wife's critical nature is the crux of the problem and is forming a coalition with the therapist as he or she confronts his wife. The husband was able to communicate nonverbally with a nod, suggesting agreement with the therapist's assessment of the wife's "problems."

Each partner of a dyad needs the a priori trust and understanding of the therapist's intent and ability to balance interventions, especially before being confronted in an individual way. Such trust is needed whether the confrontation is nurturing and supportive or points out cognitive distortion or dysfunctional behavior. With adequate preparation and education about balanced and fair approach, the therapist can confront the individual in couple therapy with a very positive result. For example:

Therapist to Wife: Can you see what you were doing in that last interaction? (*looks at the husband before an answer is given and says, "I will ask you the same question next."*)
Wife: I know I get very angry and critical.
Therapist to Husband: And what do you contribute?
Husband: I guess I do something to annoy her.

Because the wife understood that the therapist was going to ask the husband also, she was able to reflect more on her functioning and be less defensive. The client's perception of balance is essential for allowing him or her to share deeply and vulnerably.

However, balance can be lost in an intervention such as the one given above. While the therapist asked fair and just questions to both parties, the husband did not respond at the same level of insight and reflection as his wife. He did not share the same level of vulnerability or take personal responsibility for his part of the negative communication. The therapist needs to recognize that the vulnerability of the wife is being exposed and not that of the husband. Direct and supportive confrontation of the husband is necessary to establish balance. If and when the husband is reflective, the therapist might return to confront the wife. As the therapist moves back and forth between clients, she or he constantly assesses the balance of intensity, the depth of responsibility being asked of and responded with by both partners, and the partners' perception of balance. An example of balanced intensity and personal responsibility would be:

Wife: I know I have been very angry and critical over the last few days. I feel very alone and am afraid of losing you.
Husband: I understand. I keep withdrawing and going into myself in part because I have felt so rejected and hurt. I just couldn't communicate my feelings directly.

Both partners are sharing their vulnerable feelings and insights into how their behavior has influenced their partner. When such balance is achieved, deeper meanings and feelings can be explored.

INCLUSIVE LANGUAGE

If the process of therapy consists mainly of the therapist talking to each partner with little couple interaction, the therapist is probably more oriented toward individual psychotherapy. Such an orientation might lead to a loss of balance, with the therapist speaking to only one spouse at a time and failing to structure couple dialogue and conflict resolution. Also, significant time might be spent confronting one partner or the other and striving for insight in an unbalanced way. When the therapist asks questions such as, "Can you both see what is happening?" and asks them of both partners, a sense of fairness can be established. Inclusive language such as "both," "the two of you," and "similar," used to suggest mutual responsibility will often decrease the competition for who is more "right" and contribute to a systemic understanding in the couple. This kind of inclusive language helps to set the tone of mutuality in the session.

Consider the following balanced interventions, which could be used by the marital therapist to heighten the awareness of the couple.

Therapist: Can you see how you both contribute to the problem?
Can you understand what you both did to nurture each other?
The two of you are being very hurtful to each other.
Do you understand that you are both really saying, "I miss you"?

You are both very similar in the way you handle stress.

You are both competing to be heard.

Let's examine this interaction. Can you see what each of you is eliciting from the other?

Such process interventions attempt to make both partners accountable. They are not made to an individual but to both partners at the same time, thereby enhancing a balanced approach and perspective. Often such balanced interventions are used to stop negative and destructive interaction by insisting that each individual reflects on his or her own behavior.

Therapist interaction with one spouse and not the other is fraught with opportunities for miscommunication. Issues of fairness, therapist objectivity, and individual responsibility become the focus when there are beliefs that the therapist is aligning with one spouse and not with both. For example, in a therapy session both members of a couple might feel frustrated and begin to argue about how each feels ignored. If the therapist loses balance and points out that the husband is not listening and is being judgmental, the husband might become frustrated because he feels judged. He may then become more enraged or possibly never return to a session. However, if the therapist says, "Please stop; you both are right. Neither of you is hearing the other person and you both are feeling judged."; the destructive interaction is much more likely to be slowed down or reframed into a more constructive conversation. The therapist who demonstrates a balanced and impartial approach to a couple calms down the fear that each spouse holds of not being heard.

For the purpose of maintaining balance, it is helpful, whenever possible, for the marital therapist to intervene in such a way that both partners of the dyad will simultaneously look at his or her own functioning in either a destructive and unhealthy interaction or a positive, nurturing one. However, interventions addressed to one partner and not to the other can be important and effective also. Some ideas about how to maintain balance when working with individuals are discussed in the following section on Intensity and Balance.

Intensity and Balance

Applying balance in the questioning of clients and managing the timing of interventions are essential skills for the marital therapist to learn. Assessing balance in terms of the intensity and depth of questions and confrontations is a more difficult, higher-level skill to develop. The following interaction is unbalanced because the intensity of intervention with the wife is at a very different level from the one with the husband.

Husband: I'm trying as hard as I can!
Wife: But it just is not good enough. You aren't thinking through anything you are doing prior to doing it.
Husband: Well if you would help me once in a while, I wouldn't get into these predicaments.
Wife: But I don't want to help you. I want you to take the initiative.
Therapist to Wife: Do you see that you are communicating in a very unfair way?
Therapist to Husband: Try and communicate what you need without blaming.

The therapist has the concept of balance in mind but is confronting in quite an unbalanced way. The word "unfair" said to the wife differs significantly in power from "Try . . . without blaming" when said to the husband. Understandably, the wife could feel blamed by the therapist, while her husband might feel the therapist to be quite reasonable. A possible intervention to the husband to balance the somewhat harsh response to the wife might be one of the following:

Therapist to Husband: Do you see how you are also communicating unfairly? or Do you understand how you could be perceived as unfair to your wife?

The intensity of an intervention needs to be balanced in terms of the power of the confrontation or request for vulnerability and insight. It is important that the marital therapist when asking for significant revelation from one spouse also asks the other spouse. Even when the therapist feels balanced in approach, she or he never truly knows the entire impact of an individual intervention. In fact, the partners themselves might not perceive the power of an intervention until much later. Therefore, the therapist must constantly assess verbal and nonverbal responses and reactions. If defensiveness occurs in one partner, it might be the consequence of a perception that the therapist is unfair or unjust.

The immediacy of balanced intervention is also very important. In the above dialogue, if the therapist stated that she or he would like to deal with the husband's issues in the present session and the wife's difficulties in the session the following week, a number of problems could occur. The husband's vulnerabilities and responsibility for the dysfunctional couple patterns would be exposed for an entire week before the wife might have to deal with her complementary role in the couple dynamic. In that time, the husband could feel sided against and the wife could feel justified. Coalitions might be formed with friends or family that would need to be processed. The wife's responsibility in the couple's circular patterns might never be examined as the sessions become more imbalanced toward confrontation of the husband.

Balance techniques should be demonstrated within each therapeutic session, not week to week. In heated confrontation, the most effective balance might occur every several minutes. This means that the therapist orients the conversation back and forth between two partners while trying to keep the length of discussion and the depth of intervention and intensity balanced and fair.

ROOM SETTING TO PROMOTE A BALANCED SESSION

One of the simplest balancing concepts to understand, and one of the most violated, pertains to the room setting and the couple and therapist seating positions. Assessment of alignments and coalitions among any group of people can be readily ascertained by watching nonverbal cues such as who faces whom and physical proximity (Minuchin & Fishman, 1981).

Therapist balance and client perceptions of fairness and therapeutic process can be affected by the positioning of the chairs and the posture of the marital therapist. For example, suppose the therapy room is set up with the two clients directly facing the therapist, as if in a classroom, and not at all towards each other. This structure suggests that the therapist will be the leader or instructor. Implicit is the idea that the therapist's insight and direction are the important dynamic in the couple's therapy. By making it difficult for the couple to face or to speak to each other, the therapist reinforces client dependency on the therapist and inhibits the use of couple interaction to explore issues.

In seeming contradiction, this might be the exact structure a therapist uses if the clients are hostile and blaming or functioning in a highly enmeshed manner. By making the therapist central to the therapeutic process, there is more chance to stop the reactiveness of the couple than if the couple were to continue to look directly at each other. Of course, the eventual goal is to move the therapist out of the center and to increase the effectiveness of the couple interaction, while encouraging the couple to face more towards each other.

A structure in which the couple directly faces one another could, in a negative way, increase the likelihood that the clients will be enmeshed and conflictual and, in a positive way, structure an intimate communication amongst themselves with the therapist as an observer. Clients who are conflictual might independently move their chairs to face the therapist and away from each other to create more safety and less couple intimacy. The couple who has been working hard at their intimate comunication might not need the buffer or the safety that the therapist provides and move their chairs towards each other. In cases in which couple intimacy is sought, the therapist might want to take himself or herself out of the middle of the couple interaction and encourage the partners to speak directly to each other. The active therapist should certainly be able to intervene no matter what the seating arrangement.

In an initial session it is suggested that each chair be positioned equally to face the two other chairs, somewhat like the three sides of a triangle. With equal ease of conversation among clients and therapist, there is the greatest likelihood for balancing the input of the therapist with enactments and couple interaction. From this position the therapist and clients can turn their heads to make the therapist more or less central to the couple conversation.

Understanding the relationship of body language and concepts of fairness and balance is crucial for every marital therapist. When the therapist positions herself or himself towards the couple and not towards an individual, a sense of balance and fairness is created. By facing one partner and not the other feelings can emerge in the clients of being picked on or sided against or, conversely, being aligned with and being the favorite. The general body position of the therapist when not making a specific interaction should be towards the middle of the space between the clients or equally towards both partners.

Balance of eye contact is important. Looking straight at one partner by the therapist will probably engage that partner. If continually done in an unbalanced way, the therapist is communicating a number of possible things. Perhaps she or he is aligned with or against that person or is reacting in some way to the personality of the client. Whatever the reason, the most difficult effect of maintaining eye contact with one client and not the other is that the individual being stared at will find it hard to look away and could be pulled out of an interaction with his or her partner.

Eye contact should be balanced in intensity and duration with each client as much as possible. When an enactment—an opportunity for the couple to interact with each other—is being structured by the therapist, the therapist might look down. By the therapist avoiding any eye contact with either partner, the clients will find it more difficult to resist an intimate communication with each other by looking up and engaging the attention and eyes of the therapist.

Touch, if perceived to be appropriate by the therapist, should be of the same quality and nature with both partners. For instance, if the therapist shakes the hand of the husband, she or he should probably do the same with the wife. A hug offered to one partner and not to the other can create issues of injustice and feelings of alienation. Touch, in general, should emerge out of the feelings of the session and the needs of the client. When done as a habit, touch can communicate a superficial intimacy likened to a marital couple who give each other a peck on the cheek every morning.

PSYCHOPHARMACOLOGY AND BALANCE

Perhaps one of the most difficult couple interventions to be made in a balanced way is the suggestion of medication for one partner and not for the other. Medication would be for the purpose of alleviating anxiety or depression, which might affect both the individual and the health of the marital relationship. The client needing medication can be tempted to view himself or herself as the "sick one," or the spouse not needing medication may feel vindicated of personal responsibility. Every marital therapist should be versed in the effective use of medication to enhance the health of an individual, to alter a negative circular pattern of couple interaction, and for accurate psychiatric referral. Framing such an intervention for the couple, in a balanced way, takes considerable thought. Possible frames to suggest medication are:

1. "You both are contributing to the problems in ways we have dis-

covered over the last number of sessions. (*To one partner*) Some of the difficulties you are having with depression and your consequent negative feelings, I believe, could be helped with the use of medication. (*To the other partner*) On the other hand, your issues won't respond to medication and have more to do with learning and family of origin. You will have to work hard to positively influence these tendencies and personality traits. With the use of medication for you, and with both of you working on issues of family of origin, the quality of the relationship could be enhanced."

2. "I believe that medication can help you to function better and to feel less down on yourself. If that is the case, and one of you begins medication, you both will have to look at the relationship differently. (*To the partner in need of medication*) When not depressed, you might look at the actions of your spouse very differently, with less hurt or rejection. As this stops, you (*looking at the partner not in need of medication*) may have to examine some of the fears you might feel when intimacy is more of a possibility."

3. "The issues you both describe are certainly workable. I believe that about 10 to 20 percent of the difficulty has to do with the anxiety that seems to have control of you. I would like you to try medication to determine whether it can alleviate some of the symptoms. I can refer you to a psychiatrist, whom I know and respect, who can assess for the possible use of medication. I will continue to see both of you in therapy. The three of us will focus on the other 80 or 90 percent of the difficulty that the medication will not affect."

By balancing the responsibility for progress in the therapy and not making it impinge on the effectiveness of the medication, the individual will be more likely to accept the psychiatric referral for an assessment. In the last example, if the importance of medicine is put in perspective, the referred spouse is less likely to feel like a patient.

TECHNIQUES TO DETERMINE BALANCE

There are three objective means for the therapist to assess balance and level of bias. These include monitoring time, counting interchanges and who speaks to whom, and making inquiries to the client couple.

Monitoring Time

While there are almost always exceptions to any rule, a therapist unknowingly spending considerably more time with one partner versus another is often a reliable indication of transference or countertransference issues or alignment and coalitions between therapist and one or both partners. A good exercise is for a marital therapist to assess how much time is spent with each client. If 45 minutes is spent in discussion with one partner and 5 minutes with another, this might be a warning sign to the therapist that the therapy is losing its systemic foundation.

Length of time spent can also be measured for the therapist talking, the therapist talking with one spouse and then the other, conversation between the two partners, and length of silence. If the marital therapist is doing the majority of the talking, there is probably little therapy taking place. Instead, a lecture or at best some psychoeducation is dominating the process. The verbose therapist—one who does not let the clients speak—probably has little sense of the process of marital therapy. The therapist spending time both talking to the individual spouse and helping both partners engage in conversation with each other is probably facilitating a more effective marital process.

If all conversation is channeled through the therapist, she or he is probably either anxious and fears losing control or has been inducted into the resistance of the couple. Client interaction in enactments, structured by the couple and the therapist, is central to marital work. The presence of some silence in a session can be a positive indication that the therapist is asking probing questions for thought and insight or perhaps is allowing for a more profound level of feeling. Sessions filled with a constant flow of words are probably indicative of high levels of anxiety.

Counting Interchanges

Another helpful tool for determining balance is the counting of interchanges between the various participants. An excellent exercise to determine the nature of the process of a session is to listen to an audio- or videotape and count how many times each person speaks to every other person. If all dialogue is between therapist and one individual of a couple, the therapist might actually be doing individual therapy in a conjoint setting. In certain cases, such as exploring family-of-origin issues or eliciting affect, such individual therapy with both partners present might be preferable.

However, in most cases when the dialogue is predominately between an individual and therapist, the therapist does not have a clear enough understanding of the use of enactments in marital therapy. The marital therapist who is central to all conversation might have a need for control or have an overresponsible attitude for the movement and content of the session. Most often a constructive and dynamic process of marital therapy will include significant couple dialogue, therapist's comments and interventions to each individual, and process comments directed towards the couple.

Making Inquiries

Perhaps the most obvious technique for adequately assessing the balance of the therapist's approach is to ask a client couple, "How have I been balanced or unbalanced in my approach to both of you?" or "Comment on your perception of the responsibility you both are being asked to take in the marital difficulties." Clients will often feel safer with a therapist who can ask such questions because they know the therapist is thinking about issues of fairness, and they recognize that she or he is fallible and welcomes constructive feedback. If balance is lost and these statements have been made, there is a greater likelihood that the clients will verbalize their feelings before trust and confidence in the effectiveness of the therapy are undermined.

THE MEANING OF LOSS OF BALANCE

When a client feels unfairly confronted, when siding and coalitions are created that alienate one of the spouses, or when the marital therapist diagnoses a couple in cause and effect rather than systemic terms, there are a number of possibilities for the therapist to consider.

1. The therapist might lack the skill and ability to think systemically.
2. The therapist might have unresolved issues from family of origin that are being tapped by the client's content or process.
3. The therapist might be in a countertransference as a reaction to

projections from the client or in a transference, in which the therapist is projecting his or her own material onto the client.

4. The clients are not free of responsibility and might be working to get the therapist to be unbalanced so that they can exit therapy or fail to change a homeostatic pattern.

Whatever the reasons, violations of fairness, justice, and balance should prompt a therapist to discuss them with his or her supervisor or therapist or to reflect in order to understand the etiology of the imbalance of approach and then do what needs to be done to correct it.

CONCLUSION

In conclusion, balance is a central systemic concept. It is necessary for the marital therapist to develop skills to maintain a balanced and fair approach so that both individuals of a couple can examine their responsibility in the marital difficulty.

Chapter 4

Systemic Intervention

In systems theory addressing the individual as well as the context in which the individual relates is important. Systems theory delineates the interrelatedness of the family members to each other (Bowen, 1972). An ability central to systemic thinking is to differentiate linear interventions from systemic ones. Many marital therapists have never made the conceptual transition from a more linear and individual approach to one more circular and systemic. So much education is designed around an almost exclusively linear way of thinking that it is virtually impossible for some therapists to reorient their conceptual perspectives to include learning to assess and question clients in a circular manner as well. Circular epistemology is a view of reality that one event does not directly cause another as in linear epistemology. Such a model of causality is multicausal and multidetermined.

Linear thinking is based on the ability to probe for cause and effect. Such cognitive processing looks at why people act the way they do. Combinations of linear questions can develop a circular understanding of the nature of a couple's interaction. For example:

Therapist to Wife: Why do you get so angry?
Wife: Because he always withdraws from me.
Therapist to Husband: Why do you withdraw?
Husband: Because she is always so angry.

Withdrawal and anger contribute to a circular and reciprocal pattern. Singular linear questions that do not probe the interrelatedness of behavior can result in a therapist or client attributing blame by focusing the responsibility for a problem or conflict upon a single person or event. Using the above example, the wife justifies her anger on the basis of her husband's withdrawal. The linear-oriented therapist may think the same way and attempt to help the husband not to withdraw without also examining the effect of the wife's anger on the pattern of withdrawal.

This type of thinking could be diagrammed as A → B. Therefore, fix A, and B will be fine. However, it is equally valid that the wife's anger is contributing to the husband's withdrawal. Consideration of the interaction of anger and withdrawal brings the therapist from a more linear perspective to a more circular one. Linear thinking does not take into account the more complex and circular nature of human behavior and interrelationships, because it focuses responsibility in only one direction.

Systemic thinking includes cause and effect but extends the concepts to include identification of circular and reciprocal patterns. The diagramming of such patterns would be A → B → A → B ad infinitum (Penn, 1982). In systemic thinking, discovering who is at fault or who began the problem is secondary to exploring how each partner, family member, influences of family of origin, societal values, and so on contribute to the reciprocal patterns. If the client says, "I am happy because my husband is so attentive," the therapist who thinks in a systemic way will discover that the husband is attentive, in part, because the wife is happy. The feeling of happiness and resulting intimacy experienced by both partners form a positive reciprocal and circular pattern.

The therapist who thinks linearly tends to stay focused on the individual, while the systemic therapist tends to look at the relationships and processes between partners, families, and social contexts. Systemic thinking reinforces the idea that even an illness such as depression—with its "cause" perhaps rooted in psychobiology—still has enormous ramifications for spouses and family members. The role and function of the depression, and how two partners and family members respond to them, are always significant factors in marital dynamics and the depth of the depression itself.

The relationship of any behavior, emotion, or thoughtful expression to the personality of the individual, marital relationship, family, or society is always key (Pierce, Nichols & DuBrin, 1983). It is the function and purpose of behavior that can be elaborated more fully in systemic thinking. What was the behavior for? How does the behavior fit into the relational patterns? Where does the behavior come from? How was it influenced by family of origin? This chapter will illustrate linear and circular questions and techniques for the marital therapist seeking to intervene in diverse ways.

CIRCULAR QUESTIONS DEEPEN THE MEANING OF LINEAR QUESTIONS

The information elicited by circular questions extends beyond linear inquiry. For example, if the client says, "I feel depressed," linear questions might be:

1. What caused the depression?
2. What event began the depressed feelings?
3. When did your mother or father first comment on the depression?

Questions that seek a more systemic understanding might be:

1. Is anyone else in your family depressed?
2. How does your spouse respond to your depression?
3. What role does depression play in your marital intimacy?

If the client says, "I am furious!" linear questions might be:

1. What causes you to be furious?
2. When did you get so furious?
3. Who causes you to be so angry?

Systemic questions might be:

1. What does your spouse do when you are furious?
2. What is the relationship between your anger and your ability to be intimate and vulnerable?
3. Were either of your parents angry in a similar manner?

Both sets of questions are important. However, the systemic questions are going to enrich the therapist's understanding of how an individual issue is part of a couple or family pattern in ways that linear questions will not. Linear questions will give the therapist a more single-minded approach to the etiology and understandings of an individual's or couple's behavior. While finding cause can be enlightening, looking at cause as part of a more complicated set of circumstances and relationships will give the therapist more opportunity to intervene and change couple patterns. The question "Who caused you to be so angry?" will possibly lead to the identification of one person as the cause. The question "Were either of your parents angry in a similar manner?" begins the process of a client looking at family of origin, introjected patterns, and insight into how anger has affected past and current relational patterns.

CIRCULAR QUESTIONS AND BALANCED INTERVENTION

One of the primary roles of the marital therapist is to remain balanced and to demonstrate fairness by relating to both individuals of a couple. "There are two sides to every coin" and "It takes two to tango" are colloquialisms that suggest the importance of looking for shared responsibility in any marital issue or problem. When the therapist thinks linearly, it is often quite difficult to remain balanced and fair because blame can more easily be attributed to one partner. The therapist can be easily inducted into a couple's dysfunctional pattern by listening and agreeing with one spouse's description of the other's faults. By looking at the circular patterns of behavior, the actions of both spouses are taken into consideration. By extending the understanding of systemic thinking beyond the couple, the therapist seeks to encourage both partners to look at patterns of relating in family of origin and social context. The systemic assumption that nothing happens in a vacuum and that both partners should be held accountable makes balance and fairness easier to establish.

LEARNING TO THINK IN A SYSTEMIC MANNER

How does a therapist learn to think in a systemic way? Part of the answer is to look for the meaning of any behavior outside of, as well as inside of, the person exhibiting the behavior. Consider the following examples:

1. A woman client begins to cry during a conjoint therapy session. Linear thinking will lead the therapist to ask who or what caused her to cry and probably limit the inquiry to that understanding. A more systemic thinker will attempt to ascertain the function and purpose of the crying for both the individual and the system in which she relates. For instance, the therapist will notice how the spouse or partner responds to the crying. If the partner becomes angry in response to the crying, perhaps it means

more than a sharing of a sad feeling. Crying may be used to manipulate or to elicit guilt. The partner's anger may be a safer way of expressing feelings of fear or incompetence. In such a manner, the couple might create distance from each other. There are many possibilities for the meaning of crying and the response of anger within a dyad.

2. A husband grows very hostile towards his wife. Before the therapist responds or intervenes, it is crucial that she or he look over at the wife to determine her response. The nature of the response will provide the therapist with an increased understanding of the meaning and purpose for the hostility. If the woman withdraws, maybe the husband is trying to set up rejection and withdrawal. If the wife yells back in a hostile way, perhaps this is the only way that the couple stay out of depression or know how to be intimate. The man's hostility may be grounded in feelings of powerlessness. Once expressed, it may serve some personal and systemic function. The therapist can examine each partner's reaction in order to better determine the meaning of the hostility from multiple perspectives.

3. A man states, "I really feel sad." On the surface this statement seems to be assertive and quite revealing. Because the therapist thinks in a systemic way, she or he looks to the partner to see the response. To the therapist's surprise, the woman is disinterested. When asked about her disinterest, the woman states that whenever her husband wants sex later in the day, he starts to express his sadness and vulnerability early in the morning. He has a circuitous way of asking for intimacy and care. The therapist discovers that the wife is angry about her husband's indirectness. The husband asks circuitously in part because he fears his wife's anger. The couple's sadness and anger then organize in a circular fashion. Systemic interpretations can aid in the therapist's understanding of the function of a specific individual's behavior. In the above example, "I really feel sad," was not a catharsis or an attempt to share an emotion to establish intimacy, but an indirect request for sex, which was then perceived as a manipulation by the partner.

4. A husband states, "Every night when I come home from work I approach my wife and want to be very affectionate." The therapist who concludes, without inquiry, that this statement is sensitive and caring is not necessarily thinking in a systemic way. A systemic question is, "When the husband is affectionate, what does the wife do in response?" Upon further inquiry, the therapist finds that every night just before the husband

comes home, his wife becomes agitated and withdrawn. When the husband approaches, his wife wants to pull back. The affection now takes on a new meaning. The husband may be unconsciously distancing his wife because he knows that she will withdraw upon his approach. He then can criticize her unavailability and justify his own behavior. This example of one partner reaching out in a seemingly affectionate way for the purpose of distancing his partner is a common marital dynamic (Napier, 1978). The systemic therapist must be able to sit back and be enough of an observer of the couple's process to determine how a singular comment by one partner is received by the other.

5. A woman states, "I really understand how I have let you down. Please give me a another chance." The man receiving this message remains unforgiving and rigid in his response. The therapist can confront the man for not being more open by saying, "This was a clear, reasonable, and assertive statement by your wife." But what the therapist may not understand is that the woman's statement is part of a dance that the couple does together (Lerner, 1989). After the woman asks for forgiveness several times, the man finally softens and becomes more giving. As soon as this occurs, the woman disappoints the man again and he becomes enraged and rigid as the cycle repeats itself. Both spouses feel abused and rejected, which are old repetitive feelings derived from their families of origin.

Once the message sent and the answer received are understood and their interrelationship is noted, the function of a behavior can be examined as it relates to one's family of origin, to levels of differentiation with parents, to individual personality, and to self-concept. The partner who recognizes systemic patterns, their origins, and the effects on personality can take some personal responsibility to change him- or herself, the couple patterns, and other relationships in which the patterns are manifested.

SYSTEMIC THINKING LEADS TO WIDER INTERPRETATION AND INTERVENTION

Systemic thinking leads to other types of interventions that assist the therapist in his or her understanding of the intricacies of a couple's relationship and their extended family relationships. A therapist who thinks systemically assumes that behaviors of a couple are not random but intricately connected. What one partner receives from another is not by mistake and often there are some, or many, covert or overt dynamics creating patterns and responses that, positively or negatively, are of service to each individual.

In the frequently observed reciprocal patterns of anger in response to withdrawal and vice versa, one systemic intervention is to probe whether the person who is angry is unconsciously asking his or her partner to withdraw (Napier, 1990). Is the person who withdraws for some reason asking for anger or abuse? Part of the answer to such questions may be found in the early introjected feelings from the husband or wife's family background. Early introjects, if strongly negative and hurtful, can result in repetitive patterns later in life, which are unconsciously repeated with a spouse (Scharff et al., 1988). Unresolved childhood feelings often find expression in the intimacy and commitment of a marital relationship. For example:

1. Bob is an adult child of an alcoholic mother. He experienced a great deal of verbal abuse and inconsistent parenting. Overall, he felt abandoned and rejected as a child. Feelings of abandonment and hurt were introjected and once he was married were transformed into issues of abandonment within the marriage. Bob picked a woman who was also hurt in her upbringing. By being emotionally unavailable to his wife, he elicited a great deal of criticism and rejection from her. By blaming her for being emotionally distant, he repeated an old pattern and lacked understanding about his own repetitive creation. Bob did not understand the function of his critical behavior. A systemic intervention, done with good timing and with sensitivity, is to inquire about how being abandoned is predictable and perhaps keeps him safe. After gaining some understanding, the patterns of eliciting rejection in a repetitive way can be directly confronted and worked through.

2. Joan married a man who was completely unaware of his feelings. She spent a long time in the marriage trying to elicit feelings and closeness from her partner, but the more she pushed, the more he resisted. The couple came to therapy with the goal of decreasing the tension. Joan had the unspoken goal of trying to get her husband to express his feelings. Linear thinking by a therapist might encourage him or her to attempt to elicit the husband's feelings. Such change is one crucial aspect of altering the couple interaction. A systemic thinker will also ask what investment Joan has in marrying someone

so quiet and unemotional and how she overfunctions in an effort to maintain his silence and lack of intimacy.

3. A client comes to a therapist saying, "My wife left me for another man." The therapist is immediately empathic and sides with the husband's view of the distressed relationship. Systemically, however, the therapist needs to think at least in terms of what part the husband played in his wife's leaving, or at the very minimum, how he was distancing his spouse. Does this recent abandonment fulfill some old loyalty or legacy in the husband's background? Thinking systemically stimulates different ways of thinking and of conceptualizing the dynamics of the couple's interaction.

In systemic thinking, issues from family of origin reconstituted in current relationships are a key focus. A tendency exists, called homeostasis, to maintain the status quo and to organize these reconstituted patterns by keeping everything the same in a marital dyad and the family, as well as between generations. Within such repetitive patterns, another type of systemic intervention might invite insight and allow for movement. Everyone has some resistance to change. Thus, the recognition of reciprocal and systemic patterns can be very frightening for one or both partners. For instance, a wife might constantly complain that her husband is never around or is never emotionally available. If the systemic assumption that she has some investment in the distance is true, then the following interventions—either directly asked of the client or elicited through client insight—might make sense. For instance:

- Would you be scared if your husband turned to you and was emotional?
- How do you contribute to the undermining of your husband's attempts to be affectionate?
- Would you be able to feel or to see if your husband was being emotional? You seem very sure that he can't be.

A general systemic assumption is that one spouse will generally resist the movement of the other if the couple's established homeostatic patterns are challenged. Even though one partner is finally giving the other exactly what is being asked for, change can be frightening and unpredictable. Change of behavior might increase the possibility of vulnerability and intimacy. Systemic questions can point out the lack of reinforcement given to change, make clients aware of the different levels of resistance, and increase the likelihood of movement. For instance, "Would you be frightened if you received what you asked for?" "If you felt loved by your spouse, think about how you would have to change the way you think about yourself." It is part of the marital therapist's task to anticipate that what a husband and wife might want most could be what they most vehemently resist and at deeper levels fear. As small movements of change are not reinforced, and given insight, significant couple growth is thwarted.

Systemic thinking, when modeled and taught to a client couple, begins the process of the couple having some power over enhancing the quality of their relationship. Replacing the linear processes of blame and judgment with personal understanding and insight into the interrelationships of different behaviors gives the spouses the opportunity to take personal responsibility for changing the patterns in the relationship. If a husband or wife understands that withdrawal elicits anger from a wife or husband, she or he can work on the withdrawal to effect change. One definition of personal power is the ability to take responsibility for one's own functioning without projecting blame onto another. Insight into the function of behavior and the expression of thought or feeling gives an individual the tools to relate in a more powerful and effective manner.

CONCLUSION

In conclusion, it is important to understand the relationship of linear and systemic thinking and intervention. Linear thinking examines cause and effect, and systemic approaches seek to discover the meaning and function of symptoms in reciprocal and repetitive patterns of relationships. Basic to a systemic approach is the assumption that both partners of a couple, or every member of a family, are at least somewhat invested in every conflict and issue. If an individual can understand his or her contribution to a dysfunctional communication or reciprocal pattern, then she or he can be empowered towards change and growth. Within the systemic approach, circular questioning deepens understanding, helps to maintain a therapist's balance, and leads to wider interpretations and interventions than linear questions alone.

Chapter 5

Moving from Content to Process

Content consists of what is being said—the data and information. Process is the manner and intent by which the content is shared. The systemic therapist needs to be skilled in eliciting and hearing the content as well as understanding the function and meaning of the communication—the process. This chapter will discuss how to explore for and interpret the deeper meanings underlying content.

To become skilled in identifying process, the therapist needs to concentrate on developing more effective listening skills so as to uncover the "between the lines" meanings of clients' language. Concurrent with tracking the content, the marital therapist can listen for the meaning behind a certain tone of voice, the "why" of a specific word choice, and the overall intent of a message that is not fully expressed in words.

This chapter will provide some suggestions on how to become a more perceptive listener of client process. Tone of voice will be discussed as a way to control relationship intimacy and as an expression of assertiveness, aggressiveness, submissiveness, or passive-aggressive behavior. Word choice and meaning will be emphasized as focuses of therapist intervention. The goal is for the therapist to track the content while simultaneously understanding the process of the communication at a number of different levels. Common language patterns between partners will conclude the chapter.

TONE OF VOICE

Clearly, tone of voice suggests to the therapist a great deal about the intent and meaning of a communication. A difficulty for many marital therapists is that they do not confront the way something is being said, but instead respond to and elaborate upon the content of a message. However, the marital partner who is listening will often respond to tone of voice as much as to the content of his or her partner's communication. A negative tone of voice can be aggressive and invasive, creating defensiveness in the listener. Invasive language violates the ego boundaries and identity of an individual. It is langauge that is aggressive and often controlling and manipulative. For example, one spouse might say to the other,

"You never are affectionate, you are selfish and uncaring and only think about yourself. Are you listening to me?"

These types of phrases said in an angry, aggressive tone will probably feel like an attack. They are difficult for the listener to simultaneously hear and respond to without becoming defensive. In general, invasive language and tone of voice—no matter how accurate the content—will not be heard and will produce a defensive response. The content of such discussions is often misunderstood and misinterpreted. In other words, the couple can talk about many content areas in the same defensive manner and aggressive tone of voice and have the same negative result.

The marital therapist needs to confront both the tone of voice and the invasiveness of the language—that is, the defensive and aggressive attitude that probably masks deeper feelings of fear or pain—and the response or reaction of the listening spouse *before* discussing the content of a message. The confrontation could be in the form of a request: "Could you say the same thing and change your tone of voice?" or "Your tone of voice is aggressive; try and say the same thing assertively." Or to the listener: "How are you hearing what your partner is saying?" Other possibilities include asking why the communication was verbalized aggressively, or inquiring about what the aggression elicits from the partner. The intention of such interventions is to develop a process that is less reactive and more cognitive, thoughtful, and/or sharing of feeling on the part of the sender.

Another form of language that creates difficulty for the process of effective communication is, paradoxically, a tone that carries very little intensity. Passive and unassertive language is so difficult because the listener strains to hear and interpret what the communicator is trying to say. Often the result is a listener who might give up trying to understand the communicator. In this way a couple might be colluding to resist more intimate sharing.

To establish a healthy process of communication, the therapist might ask the communicator to speak louder, to intensify his or her speech, to become more assertive, or ask the listener to respond in a more assertive, less reactive manner. Inquiry into the meaning of speaking with little intensity and why the partner reacts to it may bring insight into deeper personal feelings and thoughts and couple dynamics.

Effective communication is characterized by a tone of voice that is assertive, not aggressive and is sensitive to the emotional boundaries of others. Often, there will be a reflective quality to the tone. For instance, a spouse might say,

- "I understand that I . . ."
- "I feel sad about . . ."
- "I realize that I . . ."

Clarity without force or coercion and listening with an intent to understand and not to defend are characteristics of effective communication.

WORD CHOICE AND MEANING

Client word choice and meaning constitute another area of concentration for the marital therapist. The specific words used by clients are major clues to innermost feelings and thoughts. Words that carry emotional weight or cognitive significance may well be the focus of an entire session, as deeper and more significant interpretations and feelings are sought. Such significance is evident with a client who expresses emotions in unqualified terms such as, "I am sad" instead of "I am sad today about . . ." or "I am stupid" instead of "I do not understand this." Feelings expressed in absolutes often have direct historical roots from the client's early experiences and relationships.

- "I am *always* rejected by him/her."
- "He/she has *never* loved me."
- "Why do I *always* have to take care of you?"
- "He/she abandons me *all* of the time."

When feelings are communicated in the absolute, without qualification, a therapist should delve for deeper historical significance than what is apparent in the current relationship.

The therapist must make inquiries and pursue definitions actively to clarify a client's intent and to specify meaning between speaker and listener. It is important not to assume that the partners understand each other. For example, there are many ways a therapist could respond to the client who expresses these feelings:

- I feel down.
- I feel sad.
- I feel happy.
- I am scared there is no floor.

Many therapists think they understand the meaning of these feelings without obtaining more specific explanations and descriptions for increased insight and emotional expression. Although it may seem that the content of a message is clear, the meanings behind and hidden within a communication affect the process a great deal. Much miscommunication occurs when the communicator is inadequately clear or the listener is hearing from a specific set of preconceived ideas. After the therapist shares empathy and understanding regarding how the partner is feeling, the next step could be to ask about the words "down," "sad," "happy," "scared," and "floor" to determine the deletions, distortions, and generalizations, which can help to characterize, expand, and further interpret the above expressions (Bandler & Grinder, 1975). The following illustrates this kind of inquiry:

Client: I feel down.
Therapist: Down about what?
    Down about whom?
    Can you describe down?
    How far down?
    Do you feel down some of the time or all of the time?
Client: I feel sad.
Therapist: Sad about what?
    Sad towards or about whom?
    What kind of sad?
    How deep is the sadness?

Are you sad all of the time?
Are you sad about everything?
Client: I feel happy.
Therapist: Happy about what?
Happy about whom?
How happy are you?
Are you happy all of the time?
Client: I feel scared all of the time.
Therapist: Scared about what?
Scared about whom?
At what time do you feel scared?
How scared are you?
Are you truly scared every day?

The attentive and realistic therapist will not assume understanding of a client's specific meaning, but will ask questions and share feelings to understand more deeply the intention—conscious or unconscious—of a word choice. Because language is sufficiently inexact, the therapist has to inquire as to meanings that are deleted, distortions that are present, and generalizations that exaggerate the true intention of the expressor and the response of the listener. Consider the family characterized below.

The Stewart family presented in therapy with their 12-year-old son, John, as the identified patient. John's brother Paul and his mother and father all described John as being rebellious and a trouble-maker. The therapist decided to orient part of the session around the meaning of the words "rebellious" and "troublemaker." The therapist realized that both words were packed with deletions, distortions, and generalizations, which if left hidden, would prevent the family from seeing how they had constructed a view of itself based on language and the lack of shared meaning.

Each family member was asked what these words meant. The father discounted the seriousness of his son's behavior and attributed his actions to those of a normal teenager; rebelliousness was a part of growing up. The mother interpreted "troublemaker" to mean John was heading down a path toward juvenile delinquency. Paul was jealous of the rebelliousness. For him, it meant that John could get away with so much more than he could at that age. He believed John was receiving preferential treatment. John thought that "rebelliousness" was fine and normal, especially in comparison to the actions of his peers.

The alignments and coalitions within the family structure became quite clear as the meanings of the words were elicited from the family. The therapist watched as the mother said in an angry, anxious way, "John is so rebellious and a real troublemaker," while the father laughed in a condescending fashion and as brother Paul sat in an angry sulk.

Words communicate meaning but never reveal the complete meaning. Further elaboration and intention of the communication needs to be sought by the therapist and/or a spouse who is actively listening.

COMMON LANGUAGE PATTERNS IN COUPLES

Couples develop language patterns that are important for the therapist to identify and understand. Four general patterns will be discussed: Language as a Manager of Distance; Assertive, Aggressive, Submissive, and Passive-Aggressive Communication; Reactive and Responsive Listening; and Reciprocal Language Patterns.

Language as a Manager of Distance

Language is a powerful tool that can be used to determine the amount of closeness and distance in a relationship. The therapist must listen not only to the content, but also to the intent of a specific communication by focusing on the response it elicits. This will help the therapist determine whether the communication brings a couple closer or moves them farther apart, condescends or puts down, or the opposite, places one of the partners on a pedestal.

Assertive language often brings two people closer. "I" followed by a feeling and said in a reflective or sensitive tone of voice will frequently elicit a positive response. Even a message such as "I feel angry," which could be heard defensively, said with the intention of opening communication could be received positively and increase understanding between two partners. In order to communicate assertively, the sender must feel entitled to have feelings and thoughts, to speak, to be heard, and to feel that what he or she has to say is important. There needs to be a history of feelings of safety, trust, and respect within a couple's relationship for assertive communication to occur.

Language that distances a partner is often judgmental or blaming. Such language starts with the word "you," and the intention is to project or attribute blame and responsibility onto another person. A spouse who says "You never hug me!" or "You aren't very sensitive or caring!" is ostensibly communicating a wish for closeness, but the defensive response it provokes creates distance. Separation and alienation are common outcomes in communication that unconsciously repeats early destructive patterns from one's family of origin. By harboring feelings of rejection or abandonment from the past, the spouse believes that he or she is asking for closeness but in truth is establishing distance, perhaps to protect against further pain.

The following comparison of statements illustrates how the same basic content can be used in a healing, intimate way, or in a more regressive, alienating manner to push a partner away. The first statements can increase intimacy and are congruent with a wish to be nurtured and understood. The second set will probably establish distance and are incongruent in that the spouse is starving for closeness and struggling to be heard but uses words to alienate those around him or her.

Statements probably said to establish intimacy:

- "I need you."
- "I need a hug."
- "I really want to spend some time with you."
- "I am really hurting inside."
- "I feel angry with you and want to talk."

Statements probably said to establish distance:

- "Why aren't you ever there for me?"
- "You never hug me."
- "You never spend any time with me."
- "You always hurt me."
- "Why did you do this to me?"

The therapist needs to encourage and confront clients who use distancing language and help them recognize the underlying meanings of their

communications. Perhaps a client's fear or pain contributes to the trep-
idation of being too vulnerable with a spouse. Feelings of rejection or
abandonment from family of origin or originating in the marital relationship might have helped this person to develop a defensive posture. Or
perhaps the couple might be colluding to establish distance because of
their internalized fears.

Language also can be used by a partner in an arrogant, condescending, and self-denigrating way. All three suggest underlying feelings of low self-worth in the communicator and perhaps, if believed,
in the listener. Consider this dyadic communication between a husband and wife.

Husband: Why don't you ever do it the right way!
Wife: I tried, I really tried.
Husband: I've taught you before, I don't know how many times I have
    to repeat myself.
Wife: I'll try and do better next time.
Husband: I hope so.

The arrogance of the husband and the self-denigration of the wife create distance and diminish feelings of safety in the dyad. Such language can indicate a parent-to-child dynamic in a marital relationship.
In such roles, there may be little intimacy and an absence of sexual
relations.

The process-oriented marital therapist needs to be attuned to listening
for arrogant or self-denigrating behavior. Usually, one spouse will take
an arrogant position and the other will take a complementary role of being
angry, undermined, and hurt. Fearful of intimacy, the couple might work
on this destructive communication in a collusive manner so that each
person's behavior reinforces the other. If the therapist simply listens to
the content of the message, she or he might very well side with the under-
dog against the condescending partner, without taking into account the
listening partner's passive-aggressiveness and distancing behavior. If the
therapist remains objective, she or he will recognize the patterns of
distancing—as they are collusively established by both partners—and
confront them to encourage change and to increase understanding. It is
the nature of the communication and not only the specific content of
that communication that should demand a therapist's attention and
confrontation.

Assertive, Aggressive, Submissive, and Passive-Aggressive Language

Assertive language is direct, differentiated, subjective, and without judgment. Examples of assertive language usually begin with "I" and are followed by a clear statement of feeling, thought, need, or wish. "I feel very sad." "I need you to hold me." *Aggressive* language is invasive to the ego of the listener, often characterized by projection and blame. Examples often begin with "you" and have an attacking tone of voice. "You are never there for me!" A *submissive* communication uses tentative language and is spoken by someone from a "one down" position. Examples might include a diminutive statement such as "I never can do it correctly." *Passive-aggressive* messages might at first sound quite assertive but the passive-aggressive person hides the fact that she or he shares the opposite feelings from those expressed directly. Although "I like you" sounds assertive, the statement can be interpreted as passive-aggressive when the listener leaves the room and the communicator says, "I really don't like him or her at all."

Assertive styles often facilitate the listener/spouse responding in an assertive manner. If the spouse does not, the message probably was not perceived as assertive in the first place. Aggression in one spouse often inspires aggression from the other. However, the partner might respond submissively and fearfully, passive-aggressively, or passive-resistantly. It takes a very insightful and differentiated spouse to be able to respond in an assertive, emotionally present way to a spouse who is aggressive. A submissive partner often elicits aggression. Passive-aggressiveness almost always elicits aggression or passive-aggressiveness at first and can eventually lead to frustration, so that eventually the listener/spouse does not try to relate anymore.

Submissive, aggressive, and passive-aggressive styles of communication by a husband or wife could suggest that childhood dysfunctional relationships, characterized by rejection, abandonment, or low self-worth, remain unresolved and are being repeated in the dynamics of the marital communication. The therapist who is sensitive to these patterns is able to intervene in a balanced and profound way. The therapist can confront each spouse on what she or he is actually trying to elicit from his or her partner to increase client awareness. Asking questions such as, "Can you understand what you are asking for?" or "Do you see what you are creating?" can lead to systemic understandings. The responses of both partners offer insight into the circular communication patterns of the couple.

The following process questions and statements might help improve couple communication and position clients to be more assertive.

- "Try and say it without the aggression."
- "Can you get out of the submissive position?"
- "You aren't saying what you really mean and are being passive-aggressive."

After gaining insight into the meaning and effect of a communication, a couple—with the help of the therapist—must alter aggressive, submissive, and passive-aggressive language to make messages congruent with the healthier intentions and needs of the communicator and listener.

Reactive and Responsive Listening

A person who consistently reacts tends to feel attacked, insecure, and on the defensive. Reaction is defined as "the action caused by the resistance to another action, or force; counter tendency" (Random House College Dictionary, 1975). A reactive retort resists the statements of the communicator in primarily an emotional, not thought out, and defensive way. The responsive individual has more ability to listen and seek further clarification. Response, defined as "an answer or reply," has elements of both emotion and thought and is intended to further the depth and meaning of the conversation.

A *wife states*: "You did a very poor job."
  A *reaction* . . . "I did not."
    "You did just as bad a job."
    "I don't care what you think.
  A *response* . . . "What was poor about it?"
    "What do you mean by poor?"
A *husband states*: "I don't like you."
  A *reaction* . . . "Who cares."
    "I don't like you either."
  A *response* . . . "What about me don't you like?"
    "What do you mean?"
    "Could we talk about it?"

A person who is reactive perceives attack in most direct communications. She or he defensively assumes knowing the meaning of the words used by the communicator. A responder will assume that meaning is person specific and that inquiry is important before an adequate response can be made. With a primary attitude of respect and interest, the responder seeks to build communication. In terms of reciprocal patterns, reaction breeds more aggression, while response often calms down what was originally an aggressive communication and moves it toward assertion and deeper understandings.

The therapist who listens accurately will understand that if a spouse reacts to a statement made by the other spouse, there was a perceived attack or sensitive area touched. In reactive communication the couple can get quickly enmeshed. A responsive communication, however, suggests a high level of differentiation and desire to understand the meaning of the husband's or wife's messages. Healing, forgiveness, and couple intimacy are built on the foundation of responsive, nonreactive, partners.

The marital therapist needs to interrupt the reactive communications of clients. Intervention can take many forms: for instance, awareness of the origins of the reactive patterns; insight into the emotions behind the aggression; examining the attributions of each partner, that is, what each partner thinks of the other; restructuring the seating and redirecting the focus of conversation so that the therapist is more central; and directly educating the clients about the difference between reaction and response.

Intervene

One direct technique is an experiential exercise to teach clients just how reactive they are and how difficult and rewarding responding to one another can be. For example, amidst the couple's reactive argument, the therapist can say to both clients, "You know I don't like either of you!" This will probably stop their reactive communication and surprise the couple. Before they respond, the therapist can challenge them to respond to the statement and not to react. Often clients will think this so strange that they will laugh and parlay back a reaction such as, "I don't like you either!" The therapist can tell them it is a reaction and confront them until they begin to respond. A response would be for either partner to ask something like, "What don't you like about me?" thereby going after the deletions which were left out of the original expression (Bandler & Grinder, 1975).

A positive and direct challenge is to ask a couple to respond to each other at home, especially in communications in which reactions are commonplace. Another exercise, seemingly the opposite but often achieving the same result, is to send them home with the task of seeing if they can get the other to react, and to keep score. Paradoxically, this task can encourage the couple to respond, even during overt aggression. This exercise often sensitizes clients to their reactive instincts and begins the process of more responsive communication. However, this exercise should not be used with volatile or overtly aggressive couples. It is more appropriate for couples who are able to reflect and maintain some differentiation.

Reciprocal Language Patterns

The process-oriented therapist needs to be knowledgeable and sensitive to reciprocal patterns in couple communication. With such awareness the therapist is able to anticipate and confront dysfunctional communication *before* it becomes too intense and hurtful. Several of the frequently observed patterns in communication are attack and defense, anger and withdrawal, and thought followed by feeling or vice versa.

Attack and a subsequent defense by marital partners represents a common breakdown of communication. The mistake of many therapists is to wait quietly and passively, without intervening, while the couple intensify this dysfunctional pattern.

Wife: You are never affectionate to me!
Husband: I am too. Last night I reached out to you.

This pattern of attack and defense creates distance and prevents the couple from feeling too vulnerable. The therapist who can intervene after an attack and ask the communicator to share the feeling behind the attack—or ask the listener to try to respond without defending—can begin to break into this process and aid the couple's discovery of more functional communication. For example:

Client: You are never affectionate to me!
Therapist: Can you share the feeling behind what you just said?
Client: I am feeling lonely and unloved! You are never affectionate to me!
Therapist: Try not to react or defend, but respond.
Client: Let's talk about what you mean.

Such interventions by the therapist provide the possibility for breaking the destructive communication and replacing it with one that is functional. It may require great persistence to change a spouse's attacks into the more primary feelings of hurt, rejection, or powerlessness. If the therapist intervenes in a couple's reciprocal pattern in order to change reactions into responses, she or he must not be passive, but forthright and determined.

Another circular pattern frequently demonstrated by couples in therapy is vulnerability in one partner creating a reluctance in the other to share negative feelings or thoughts, and the subsequent lack of sharing resulting in further vulnerability in the other partner. A husband and wife caught in a dysfunctional communication might justify their behavior by saying:

- "Of course I feel vulnerable; he never shares anything with me."
- "Of course I hold back; she is always emotional and acting vulnerably."

An inducted therapist is one who sides with one partner against the other and listens to or confronts the accusations of one spouse, and not the other. In contrast, a systemic therapist tries several techniques to break the self-justification cycle. For instance, making a straightforward request that the clients take responsibility for their own behavior and recognize how one behavior elicits the other and can begin to break the pattern. Another helpful technique is to model self-justification and blame so that clients can hear what these sound like. The therapist can say, "My husband/wife and I had a huge fight last night and it was entirely his/her fault. I was blameless." If said in a lighthearted manner, the client often hears the one-sided nature of the accusation and begins to reflect.

The therapist who is sensitized to process issues will recognize that no behavior exists in a vacuum. When anger or withdrawal is expressed by one partner, the therapist needs to look for the response or reaction in the other and to determine the interrelationship.

CONCLUSION

In conclusion, reciprocal patterns of communication are universal in couples. The therapist who recognizes these patterns and their circular nature can systemically intervene to isolate individual responsibility, reframe and deepen insights and feelings, and help couples break destructive patterns. Such intervention must be at the level of content and process. The content is important to give insight and orient the therapist to the correct topic areas. Attention to the process deepens the understanding of the feelings and thoughts behind the overt communication and helps the therapist gain a deeper knowledge and capacity to confront or inspire the couple's negative or positive systemic patterns.

Chapter 6

Building and Managing Intensity

In couples therapy, personal growth and integration are most enhanced by a dynamic process in the treatment. Aspects of such a process include active interaction, feedback, humor, confrontation, empathy, a full range of emotions, and intellectual sharing. The systemically oriented therapist attempts to create appropriate emotional intensity among clients and between a couple and the therapist. Too much intensity can create an inability for a therapist to intervene in a constructive manner and for a couple to communicate effectively. Too little intensity can cause a therapeutic session to lack focus and prevent a couple from truly engaging each other in an intimate way. This chapter will discuss the management of intensity for the purpose of creating a dynamic therapeutic environment for clients. In addition, the often observed phenomenon of therapist and client resistance to heightening emotional intensity will be reviewed.

The therapist working with couples needs to have skills to build intensity and relatedness within a session so that the couple will generalize the cognitive and emotional experience outside of therapy in their everyday relationship. Generating intensity within a couple's therapy session requires sensitivity to process issues and the ability to use cognitions and emotions in the couple-therapist interaction.

The fundamental concept is that therapy is a dynamic process not to be reduced to an intellectual dissemination of information. When the session becomes limited to rational thought and the passive reception of information, an individual will have difficulty integrating what she or he feels and applying insight into personal experience. Emotion can be a strong motivator of change in behavior and interaction in marital therapy. However, the goal is not simply catharsis. Cognitive change will often follow emotional change, and emotional change, of necessity, involves change in cognition and action related to the emotion (Greenberg & Johnson, 1986a).

If a couple come to therapy with little affect or intensity, what could be done? How does a marital therapist turn seemingly meaningless small talk at the beginning of a session into energized, focused conversation? How can the disorganized ideas frequently contained in a client's description of the presenting problem be transformed into insight, primary emotion, and behavioral change? Conversely, how does a marital therapist work with too much couple intensity that prevents any thoughtful communication?

Bugental's conceptualization of therapist skills into "four octaves" in responding to client sharing gives the reader a thorough description of how to manage intensity and facilitate joining, trust, depth, emotional and cognitive sharing, and structures for change (Bugental, 1987). These octaves consist of four major areas of therapist aptitude: (1) various listening skills; (2) guiding and focusing; (3) instructing and teaching; and (4) requiring or confronting.

The last point of the first octave is also the first point of the second octave. The listening skills outlined by Bugental include the use of silence, bridging statements such as "I see," and restating, summarizing encouraging talking, reflecting the obvious, inviting expansion, and asking open questions. The second octave begins with open questions, selecting a part on which to focus, sharing factual information, structuring information, pointing out alternatives, general structuring for how much focus a specific idea should take in a session, suggesting topics, and asking moderately focused questions.

The third octave on instructing and teaching begins with asking moderate questions, rational advising, supporting, reassuring, teaching, weighing alternatives, limiting direction, and narrowing the questions. The fourth octave on requiring or confronting discusses narrowing the questions, urging on the client, approving, challenging, reinforcing or disapproving, superseding, commanding, and, only in rare cases, rejecting the client.

Four more strategies that further help to sharpen focus and create and manage intensity will be discussed: (1) specific uses of images and analogies; (2) description of emotional interventions; (3) use of repetition; and (4) the importance of the therapist focusing on primary material. The chapter will conclude with observations on the management of highly enmeshed clients who communicate with destructively high levels of emotional intensity.

(1) USING IMAGES AND ANALOGIES

In most cases, superficial expression of emotion or intellectual discussion can be transformed into dynamic interaction through a client's or therapist's use of images and analogies. Although thought and the written word can certainly carry intensity, images and analogies usually increase the depth and the energy of an interaction. As Napier (1990) wrote on metaphors, "It is in this way that our reality is transformed. A cluster of circumstances awakens in us feelings that become so charged and intense that they literally change what we are experiencing" (p. 2). A marital therapist can use images and analogies in several ways: for more accurate diagnosis, for disclosing deeper meanings and encouraging behavioral change, and for teaching different marital and family therapy concepts without the use of professional jargon.

Diagnostically, images and analogies are crucial for the assessment of the depth and seriousness of the disorder. If a female client states that she is feeling very depressed, description through analogy can be very elucidating. Besides asking the client to describe the depression in feelings and thoughts, the therapist might ask for specific analogies to further describe the depth of the depressive feelings or possible suicidal ideation. The following examples will describe less critical to more serious feelings of depression. In this example, the bottom of the hierarchy might very well prompt the therapist to consider hospitalization of the depressed individual. The client might state, "My depression is like . . ."

- a mist that dulls all the colors around me.
- walking in mud; it takes so long to get anywhere.
- a huge hole in which I am holding on to the sides.
- a black cloud that is hovering over my head wherever I go.
- there is no floor beneath me, and I am free-falling out of control.

The use of analogy is actually a projective device providing another view of innermost feelings and thoughts.

Diagnosis of the depth and intensity of anxiety and the possible need for medication are also improved by the use of images and analogies. After one male client stated that he felt very anxious, the therapist asked, "Can you tell me what the anxiety is like? What does it look like or feel like or sound like?" Consider the following hierarchy of responses which, along with other corroborating data, might indicate the seriousness of the symptoms. "Anxiety is like . . ."

- an uneasy feeling which comes and goes.
- having an unsettling feeling of danger all of the time.
- having uncontrollable negative thoughts.
- being part of a crowd trapped in a fire.

Differentiating the situational or more global character of the symptom will help the therapist determine the seriousness of a client's depression or anxiety. "I sometimes . . ." is different from "I am always." Absolutes such as "always," "never," "constantly," "incessantly," and "consistently" are clearly of higher concern than more qualified words such as "rarely," "sometimes," "occasionally," and "sporadically."

Images and analogies are helpful in understanding deeper meanings. One of the greatest mistakes a therapist can make is to assume knowing what the clients are trying to say and therefore not seeking further elaboration or clarification. The client's intellectual statement can be transformed into a more dynamic and meaningful expression when the therapist inquires about images or examples. (Further discussion in Chapter 5 on Moving from Content to Process)

The types of questions asked by the therapist are important for building intensity. If the client says, "I feel very hurt," the comment carries intensity and meaning, but may be a hint of deeper feeling only. The therapist needs to follow up on such a comment by inquiring further. "The surface structure the client has presented is incomplete, the next task is to help the client recover the deleted material. The most direct approach is to ask directly for what is missing" (Bandler & Grinder, 1975, p. 63). The questions below illustrate how the therapist might inquire:

- About whom or what are you hurt?
- Can you describe the depth of the hurt?
- What is the hurt like?
- Can you compare the hurt to an earlier experience?

- What kind of hurt?
- Give me an image that describes the feeling?

A client might state in an intellectual manner that she or he feels very angry. The therapist can inquire . . .

- About whom or what are you angry?
- What is the anger like?
- Does the feeling come and go, or is it always with you?
- In what part of your body does the anger live?
- Can you draw or describe a picture of the anger?
- How does the anger sound inside of you?

Such inquiries can help the therapist and client understand that there is no universality of meaning in behavior, and that inquiry for further depth of understanding is a necessity. With the use of images and enhanced descriptions, the intensity of a session can increase and carry more meaning for clients and therapist.

Both meaning and intensity are enhanced when intellectual concepts can be translated into image and experience. One task of the beginning therapist is to translate all of the concepts of the various schools of thought into everyday experience and example. For most clients, the use of marital and family therapy concepts and jargon during a session is not very helpful. Telling the client that she or he has been "triangulated" for years in a "fused relationship" where little "differentiation" has taken place probably will be misunderstood. To gain a better understanding of the richness and depth of marital and family therapy concepts, the therapist should work on creating images and analogies for the client. This language will raise the intensity and understanding of a particular couple's difficulty. Consider the following theories and concepts that have been transformed into insight and analogies more descriptive and applicable for use with clients.

Enmeshment or fusion is like . . .

- two people who hug in the diving area of a pool.
- two trains going in the same direction, on the same track; the speed of one is often determined by the speed of the other.
- two people shaking hands and not letting go.
- going scuba diving and sharing the same tank.

Being differentiated is like . . .

- being 30 years old and asked by your mother to get a haircut for the family picture and responding, "I do need one, I'd be glad to."
- holding onto yourself and your opinion when it seems that everyone around you wants to convince you of something else.

Lack of boundaries is like . . .

- contiguous backyards with no fences or markers; no one knows where to stop mowing their lawn.
- an inexperienced painter using watercolors.

Effective boundaries are like . . .

- fences with doors that are controlled from the inside.
- having the freedom to invite someone over and asking them to leave when you are tired.

Rigid boundaries are like . . .

- building a castle with a moat and no drawbridge.
- not letting new information cloud decisions of the past.

Intimacy is like . . .

- two swimmers, who swim together in a synchronized way for awhile, and then in an individual way swim apart.
- wanting to understand and take care of the feelings of your partner.

Positive entitlement is like . . .

- a father giving a child permission to go further in education than he did.
- a green light.

Negative entitlement is like . . .

- a red light

- when the final paper of the final class for your degree cannot quite be finished.

Such examples are as numerous as a therapist's and client's experience and imagination. Through images and analogies the theories and concepts that organize, explain, and/or describe the clients can be communicated in ways that are comprehensible.

(2) CREATING INTENSITY AND FOCUS

When the beginning therapist is taught to track the content of a client's communication, she or he needs to learn to listen to the specific words and language used by the client. Inquiry and/or comment by the therapist should attempt to mimic and focus upon the language of the client. For instance, if the client states that she or he had a bad week, the therapist could ask, "What made the week bad?" By repeating the use of the word "bad" and not changing it to a word of the therapist's choice, a client can continue to elaborate with deeper personal explanation or meaning, without having to interpret the therapist's particular meaning placed on the word choice.

If the therapist were to ask, "Why was the week awful?" the meaning of the client's emotional word "bad" might be lost in trying to interpret or resist the therapist's use of "awful." By focusing on the client's language, the therapist can show respect for the client's view and interpretation of reality, instead of immediately superimposing another. Consider the following two dialogues, one in which the couple's understandings are consistently translated into the therapist's word choice and one in which the couple's understandings were honored and enhanced.

Dialogue 1

Husband: We seem to be fighting all of the time.
Therapist: What are your arguments about?
Wife: We don't really argue. We just walk away from each other.
Therapist: Why do you both withdraw?
Husband: I feel very angry.
Wife: I don't withdraw. I just need a little time to gather myself.

Therapist: What do you think you are scared about?
Husband: I'm not really scared. I am just discouraged.

Dialogue 2

Husband: We seem to be fighting all of the time.
Therapist: Tell me about the fighting.
Wife: We both get very hurt and walk away.
Therapist: What kind of hurt? How do you walk away from each other?
Husband: For me it is a very deep hurt, a feeling of rejection.
Wife: While I do walk away, I feel more panicked and want to run.

By using the meaning and the language of the clients, a natural flow is created that increases the focus, intensity, and emotional depth of a session. If the therapist constantly transforms the client's language, the client has to work to interpret the therapist's particular meanings and the conversation becomes very disjointed.

Sharing of feeling in a natural and open way is another technique used to enhance the depth and intensity of a session. Consider the following feeling responses to a couple's pain:

Husband: We seem to be fighting all of the time.
Therapist: I'm sorry.
　　　That makes me sad.
　　　How discouraging.

Emotional expression followed by silence often will allow the client to continue the description of the fighting as she or he feels that the therapist is emotionally present. Such expressions from the therapist often have a greater likelihood of tapping into the feeling of the clients than does a more cognitive inquiry.

A client came to therapy depressed and very angry that his wife of 48 years had Alzheimer's disease. The session began with the typical question and answer format. Questions were asked such as:

• How long has she been ill?
• What has it been like for you?

- How do you cope with the difficulties?
- What did the doctor say is the prognosis?

The client dutifully responded to each question, but became more depressed and angry about his situation as the session developed. What could the therapist offer? As the therapist stopped thinking about what question to ask next, he eventually expressed that he too was angry about the client's wife and that he was experiencing such pain. The session ended and the client made an appointment for the following week.

At the next session, much to the surprise of the therapist, the man appeared considerably more at peace and less depressed. The therapist remained silent as the client said, "When I came in last week I felt alone and very angry. When I heard your anger, I realized that I was not alone and I felt better."

The angry feelings of the client were normalized by the therapist's sharing of his anger. Through the therapist's normalization of the client's feelings, other emotions of loneliness, guilt, and fear were calmed and given expression.

Silence is perhaps one of the most effective techniques for enhancing the intensity of the client's statement. This is true especially when it is connected to a nonverbal indication that the therapist is present and emotionally available. For example:

Wife: I am really hurting!
Therapist: (*leans forward, unfolds his or her arms, and says nothing*)
Wife: He doesn't seem to care about me.
Therapist: (*empathetic expression*)
Wife: (*tears*) I feel all alone!

As the therapist was perceived to be quiet, and emotionally present, the client allowed herself to become more open and vulnerable. Silence and an engaged body posture by a therapist will probably do more to elicit the emotion of the client than any inquiry. Silence can create a vacuum and permission for the client to go deeper into hurt and pain.

(3) USING REPETITION TO CREATE INTENSITY

The therapist's use of repetition can provide focus and a conceptual orientation that clients have trouble resisting. Insights and questions intended to lead the client towards more depth of feeling and vulnerability can be very difficult for the client to hear. Resistances and defense mechanisms can interfere with listening. There is often a highly developed collusion process within the couple which results in their not understanding or responding to the therapist's attempts to facilitate change. Repetition can raise the intensity of the therapist's intervention. In the following communication, the marital therapist is making a systemic intervention that is difficult for the husband to hear.

Husband: My wife is never there for me; she avoids me constantly.
Therapist: Is it possible that you contribute to your wife's avoidance?
Husband: I don't. She is always off with her own friends.
Therapist: How do you help create the distance in the relationship?
Husband: It doesn't start with me. She leaves and then I react.
Therapist: You'll be better able to change the pattern if you can figure
     out how you help create the distance.
Husband: My wife says that I am angry all of the time.
Therapist: Is that how you contributed to the distance?
Husband: I know I push her away when I get very hurt.

This last statement by the husband was his first reflective one, and it is the one that will begin the process of changing the circular patterns of the couple. Once the husband stops focusing on his partner and instead reflects on his own functioning and contribution to the problem, he begins to become individually powerful, that is, he can alter his behavior. It was the repetition that helped break through the husband's resistance.

In the next example the repetition of the client's words creates a helpful confrontation to the client's distorted way of thinking.

Wife: I simply am not smart enough to take that job.
Therapist: You aren't smart enough?
Wife: I am sure I'm not.
Therapist: I didn't realize that you weren't very smart.
Wife: Well I am not stupid!

Therapist: However, you are probably correct that you need to have more intelligence to take that job.
Wife: I might be able to do it.
Therapist: I think that you will have to be smarter.

By repeating and exaggerating the cognitive distortions of the client she was able to begin the process of altering her thinking.

Frequently, a beginning therapist does not trust himself or herself or have the personal confidence in his or her systemic interventions. When encountering client resistance, systemic interventions can be abandoned too quickly. Repetition can communicate that the therapist is focused and confident that another way of looking at things can be achieved.

(4) FOCUSING ON PRIMARY MATERIAL AND DEVELOPING A THEME

Because the deeper issues of a couple are often painful and threatening, the real sources of their distress remain hidden behind a veil of repression and denial (Napier, 1990). In order to protect the vulnerability associated with such distress, a couple can present many topics and issues to the therapist. The intensity of a therapeutic session is lost when the couple and/or the therapist allow for many issues or topics to be covered. Such avoidance can take two predominant forms: one is client focused and one is initiated by the therapist.

As was mentioned above, marital patterns are resistant to change. One of the primary ways a couple have to resist and thwart movement is to bring up many topics, change the focus of the conversation when it becomes too intense, and generally detour the therapist away from the most meaningful material. As a client communicates the broader picture, intensity can be raised if the therapist focuses on a singular idea or feeling within that picture. Generally speaking, almost any focus is better than none at all. The easiest way for the therapist to know whether he or she is focused enough is to discuss the important aspects of a session to another therapist. If the therapist cannot summarize the essence of a therapeutic session in a couple of sentences, then there was probably not enough focus.

Consider the following communication by a couple:

Wife: You are never available to me. I have to keep begging for some affection.

Husband: I feel closed in. You are always on my back.

Wife: The children need you home, not off somewhere else all day. Last weekend you watched football.

Husband: I work very hard and deserve to spend time on my own.

This couple expressed variations of these themes many times, which further entrenches the negative feelings in their relationship. The therapist who is seeking to create a focus might initially say:

- Let us focus on . . .
- What you just said is very important.
- Let us spend the rest of the session on this topic.

Possible topics to focus on are . . .

- The distancing patterns of the couple.
- The meaning of the words "begging" and "closed in."
- Exploration of patterns in family of origin.
- A discussion of time alone, time together.
- The understanding of intimacy dances.
- The role of entitlement.
- Issues of parenting.

The important factor is that the marital therapist or couple pick one topic and to pursue it in depth. Deeper meanings explored in one area will almost always generalize to other important issues and concerns.

A lack of focus initiated by the therapist is reflective of the worst understanding and application of what a therapist might call an "eclectic approach." In such "eclecticism," a therapist knows a little about each school of thought, but not enough to actually orient his or her thinking and intervention. Without such focus the therapist will often confront superficially or be inducted into the resistance of the couple.

An excellent exercise for the marital therapist is to listen to the content of what a couple present in therapy and to practice conceptualizing the material into a specific school and approach. Interventions can become more focused and purposeful once the clients' patterns can be conceptualized by the therapist. In the following examples, excerpts from client conversation are organized within different approaches. Each client statement can be organized into and understood from several theoretical perspectives.

1. *Client*: "My mother just walks into my house without even knocking."
   Conceptualization—This could be a boundary problem, best approached Structurally.
2. *Client*: "My daughter wakes up every night and I bring her into my bed."
   Conceptualization—This might be a reinforcement issue and should be appoached Behaviorally.
3. *Client*: "Every time we talk, we end up in a huge argument. We both get so defensive."
   Conceptualization—This couple might have few communication or conflict utilization skills and should work with Communication theory and practice.
4. *Client*: "I am not very smart or competent in most things."
   Conceptualization—These could be "automatic thoughts" which need to be addressed from a Cognitive perspective.
5. *Client*: "When I go home for the holidays, I seem to lose myself and get furious with my family."
   Conceptualization—This might be a differentiation issue which needs to be looked at from a Bowenian perspective.
6. *Client*: "I don't know why I have the attitudes I do."
   Conceptualization—This could be a loyalty or a legacy issue which needs to be approached Contextually in the family of origin.
7. *Client*: "I don't know why I push away the people whom I most want to love me."
   Conceptualization—This could be a matter of early introjected patterns repeated compulsively which needs to be understood from an Object Relations perspective.

The list of examples is endless. The therapist needs to be able to organize the scattered information from the couple into concepts and theories that allow for both understanding and direction for change. If the therapist is conceptually focused, more energy for change and insight can be derived from specific intervention.

MANAGING TOO MUCH INTENSITY

Too little intensity is often boring for both client and therapist. A lack of intensity can be resistance-based and prevent movement from taking place. Too much intensity can be very intrusive, destructive, and counterproductive. Clients sometimes choose a marital therapist on the basis of their perception of the therapist's ability to manage their intensity and stop potentially destructive communications. The therapist needs to have the confidence to halt negative interactions. Without such confidence, the therapist's inclination might be to structure sessions with his or her ideas instead of allowing the couple's emotions to truly emerge. The less confidence the marital therapist has, the less likely she or he is going to enhance couple interaction and to let the couple discuss their issues with the accompanying emotions.

Four techniques for managing the intense interactions of a couple are: (1) process questions that demand the couple's reflection and insight; (2) emotional interventions that seek the expression of primary feelings; (3) structuring a couple's conversation; and (4) changing the structure of the therapy. The following types of interventions are designed to manage the intense and judgmental communications of a couple.

(1) *Process questions* are designed to help the couple observe and reflect upon their own communication by helping them to become more thoughtful—hence less emotional and reactive—and objective observers of themselves. The therapist might ask:

• Is this what goes on at home?
• What is the purpose of the arguing?
• Do you want to get this out of control?
• Can you see what you are both doing?

(2) Certain *emotional interventions* take the focus off the anger and judgment of the couple interaction and redirect the discussion into more primary feelings of pain, hurt, or rejection. A therapist might say:

• This is very painful to watch.
• Please don't hurt each other like this.

- I really feel the pain behind both your angers.
- Talk about the underlying feeling.

(3) *Stronger confrontations and structuring the discussion* to lessen intensity might be:

- Stop!
- I'm not going to let you do this!
- Don't speak!
- I want one of you to share and the other to listen.
- Start with "I" and try and leave out all of the attack.

(4) *Changing* the structure of a session helps clients avoid becoming more enmeshed by stopping the interaction or moving the therapist into the center of the couple's interaction. The therapist might say:

- I am going to end the session now. It is too destructive.
- I am going to speak to one of you and then the other while insisting the other partner does not respond.
- Would you please step out of the office for a minute.

The general rule is that the more destructively intense a couple are, the more central to the process the marital therapist needs to be. Such a couple need the therapist to actively take control and calm the system.

Anticipating the depth of intensity before it gets out of control is an important skill. One of the greatest blocks for many therapists to overcome is to dissuade themselves about what constitutes being polite. In a destructive communication between clients, it is not polite to wait until one of the partners is finished speaking. A five-minute husband/wife diatribe that keeps the therapist waiting for his or her turn can set the tone for the entire session and derail efforts to be helpful. It is often effective for the marital therapist to interrupt, cut off, and prevent a client from finishing saying hurtful and destructive things. Below are two examples:

(1) The "polite" therapist . . .

Husband to Wife: I'm upset with what you did. You really are insensitive to my needs. You never once asked me for what I wanted . . . as a matter of fact, you never have and you are always selfish! You are a real bitch!

Therapist: How are you feeling?

(2) A "not polite" therapist who anticipates an evolving destructive interaction . . .

Husband to wife: I'm upset with what you did. You really are—
Therapist: Your feelings are important, however, can you share them
    without attacking, and instead share what you want or need.

The therapist can then prevent expressions of aggression or judgment by intervening directly and quickly during an escalation of anger or hostility.

The levels of intensity and their management in a therapy session are usually determined by the therapist's confidence and ability to remain detached from the affect of the client so that she or he is aware of the subtle communications and process issues. As mentioned previously, the more self-respect the therapist has, the easier it is for him or her to trust interventions and follow through.

How anger is dealt with and processed in one's family of origin and the level of differentiation of the therapist are key issues. Differentiation includes the ability to separate the emotional and intellectual processes. Someone who is differentiated is flexible, adaptable, and independent of others. She or he can cope with the stresses of life (Bowen, 1976). If the therapist's family had the extremes of too little affect or too much intrusive arguing, the therapist might be greatly limited in his or her ability to manage intensity during a session. If anger was not allowed or punished, or conversely if anger was rampant, a therapist could have a distorted reaction to client anger. Without adequate work on his or her own differentiation, a therapist will find it difficult to confront the collusion of an enmeshed couple's destructive communication and reframe it and remold it into something more positive.

CONCLUSION

The management of intensity is an important part of marital therapy. Too much emotional energy can create destructive dynamics and enmeshment. Too little energy can prevent change, behavioral application of new ideas, and couple intimacy. Managing intensity is an essential skill for the marital therapist to develop.

Chapter 7

Individual Therapy and Systemic Intervention

For a period of time in the 1970s and 1980s many therapists in the field of marriage and family therapy insisted that for therapy to be effective all members of the family should be present. Currently, working with subsystems (e.g., parental subsystems, marital dyads, and individuals as part of a family system) is more widely accepted. If a system consists of the interaction of a group of individuals—and theoretically every individual affects the system—then it follows that working in a systemic way with an individual can alter the destructive reciprocal patterns within the couple or family of which the individual is a member. Many marital and family therapists have individual clients working on systemic issues as a significant proportion of their case load. In many cases, spouses refuse to enter the therapeutic process or individuals report that they want to work in therapy by themselves.

The therapeutic task is to address personal issues systemically. If approached systemically, individual therapy can help the client to become more constructively powerful and differentiated within his or her family, as well as to leave open the possibility that a spouse or other family members might become involved in the therapeutic process at some future time.

This chapter will explore the difficulties and opportunities for the marital therapist working with an individual member of a marital dyad or with one person of a committed relationship. The ethical implications of aiding the growth of one partner without directly working with the other, combined with an understanding of the potential danger of the role of empathy when used to align with one partner against the other, will be discussed. In addition, specific consideration will be given to the therapist's role of encouraging client self-responsibility and the development of personal power. Finally, the intermingling of individual and couples therapy will be discussed.

ETHICAL IMPLICATIONS OF INDIVIDUAL THERAPY

Unwittingly, individual therapy may exacerbate couple conflict and contribute to divorce. By encouraging and enhancing one partner's growth without paying adequate attention to its effect on the partner, the therapist can unbalance and disrupt the homeostasis of the couple system (Gurman & Kniskern, 1981a). Clearly, this growth could be positive or negative depending on the many perspectives of the persons involved.

Every individual issue or concern has systemic and relational ramifications for an individual client who is part of a committed relationship. For instance, if a spouse is depressed, one systemic question that needs to be addressed is what role the depression plays in the couple's communication and overall relationship (Jessee & L'Abate, 1985). There are several possibilities. One partner, through the process of overidentification, might be experiencing depressive feelings similar to those found more severely in his or her partner. Perhaps the nondepressed partner colludes in deepening the feelings of depression in the other through criticism or withdrawal. For example, when one partner is depressed, there is little chance that the couple will be physically intimate or emotionally close. Often such collusion is derived from fears of intimacy and vulnerability.

Another possibility is that if one spouse is depressed, there is less likelihood that she or he will have the energy to leave the relationship. The less depressed partner, feeling fear of loss and a poor self-concept, knows this and unconsciously reinforces the depressive feelings. Whatever the presenting problem, whether it be anger, anxiety, weight, unemployment, self-punishment, or intimacy fears, each individual's behavior and subsequent dynamic has a multitude of systemic ramifications and possibilities.

The marital therapist working with the individual member of a dyad has an ethical responsibility to share the fact that personal growth and change, which may be enriching and constructive for him or her, might very well be debilitating or destructive for the marital or family relationships. When one spouse changes, the couple's reciprocal patterns will change and the spouse will eventually have to readjust, or alienation might ensue. If the client understands the potential harm to the homeostatic balance of the marital dyad, and still chooses to continue individual work, the therapy can continue. The marital therapist might say, "If you decide to work in therapy, you might grow or change perspectives. If you examine these issues in the absense of your spouse, it might create tension, dissension, and general distance in your marriage."

Although being empathic with the individual coming to therapy to work on marital issues is essential, it can also be problematic because of its potential to create tension and chaos within the marital dyad. By *not* being emotionally involved in the dysfunctional interactions of the marriage, the therapist can often be perceived as being more patient, caring, and understanding than either of the spouses. "Why can't my husband be more like you?" "Why can't my wife be as sensitive as you are?" Such statements should prompt the therapist to explain that she or he is not perfect and has difficulty and successes in his or her own relationships.

The therapist might share some fallibility and personal history to decrease an exaggerated positive transference. The therapist might go on to say,

> One of the goals in my listening and caring for you is that you learn that you are entitled to be treated well. You need to learn to ask for what you need in more effective ways within your marriage.

The therapist needs to be careful not to make unilateral interpretations, one-sided and linear, based on being empathetic to one partner's explanation of the difficulty. For example, a woman comes to therapy with marital issues, looking for support and understanding. The dialogue is as follows:

Wife: My husband is totally insensitive to my needs.
Therapist: What does he do?
Wife: He yells and swears at me. He comes home late and never helps around the house.
Therapist: It sounds awful.

Such empathy from the therapist, which sides with one partner against the other, can be very destructive for the future of the therapy and for the stability of the marital relationship. Because of this unilateral interpretation, the systemic framework is lost. What the therapist did not know or predict is that the woman goes home after the therapy session and shares with her husband something like the following: "I talked with the therapist today and he thinks that what you do to me is really awful." The same week the husband went to his therapist and said:

Husband: I am very frustrated and alone.
Therapist: What is happening?
Husband: My wife refuses to get a baby-sitter and the baby is sleeping in the bed with us.
Therapist: It must be difficult. She is probably overattached to the children.

In this case, what the therapist did not understand is that the husband went home to his wife and said: "The therapist thinks you are overly bonded with the children and you need to give me more attention. The therapist was very understanding of how I feel."

Through such examples of empathy and unilateral interpretations, the therapist can support each spouse to be more self-justified, less reflective, and less understanding of the feelings of the other. Then each spouse might triangulate the therapist into a coalition against the other. Neither partner at this point, in either therapy process, is cognizant of the systemic issues of circular causality, self-responsibility, and fairness. Circular causality involves the feedback model of causality in which a circular process is involved. The so-called cause is really an effect of a prior cause. What is initially defined as an effect becomes the cause of yet a later event (Watzlawick, Beavin, & Jackson, 1967). With such cautions in mind, the therapist's empathy for a client is very important.

The context for the expression of empathy in an individual session focusing on marital issues needs to be structured and well thought-out. Empathy is essential for joining with the client and establishing a context for trust, openness, and hope. However, empathy needs to be balanced with systemic interventions, such as requesting that the client take personal responsibility for contributing to the couple's circular patterns and for making bilateral or systemic interpretations—interpretations that examine the interrelationship and reciprocal nature of behavior. Again, along with empathy for the client must come a request to take responsibility for how she or he is contributing to the marital discord being described; for example, "Can you see how your behavior is intensifying the difficulty?"

In conclusion, while empathy is essential for the client-therapist relationship in the development of a therapeutic alliance, it can be problematic when the therapist is deemed to be more empathic than the spouse, it can align one spouse and the therapist against the other spouse, and it can inhibit reflection when personal responsibility is not encouraged also.

THERAPEUTIC BOUNDARIES

Another area for consideration in working with one partner of a dyad concerns the issue of boundaries. Reporting the substance and process of a therapy session to the spouse can be very counterproductive to therapeutic goals. The following two suggestions help to inhibit the inadvertent, inappropriate use of therapy material in the marital relationship.

The first idea is to establish the contract and the boundaries of the therapy during the intake session. The therapist might say to the client, "It is very important that you do not say to your spouse, 'The therapist said . . .' or 'My therapist feels that you are. . . .'" When a client triangulates a therapist in this way, the therapy can be used to gain a one-up position. A destructive coalition is formed between client and therapist which creates animosity and may result in an attempt by the absent spouse to denigrate the therapist. If the partner feels a comment by the therapist is important to share, then this idea should be integrated within the person's self and communicated as his or her own. Instead of saying "The therapist thinks," the spouse would say, "I believe" or "I have been feeling. . . ." The spouse's response can then be focused on his or her partner and the therapist is not destructively triangulated into the marital discussion or relationship.

The second reason to boundary an individual session concerns lessening the energy of therapy and detracting from the potential power of a therapeutic intervention. For example, if a therapist confronts a husband by saying, "You are judging your wife for imperfections and weaknesses in yourself." What the husband should do is integrate this thought into his own thinking and have it make sense (or not) for himself. He should process the thought privately until he understands its truth or lack of truth when applied to self-understanding and personal experience.

Instead, the husband went home and said without thinking, "The therapist thinks I'm judging you for weaknesses in me." The wife was not sophisticated psychologically and doubted the validity of the statement.

She found it had no relevance for their relationship. "That is ridiculous," she said. The husband, who sought validation and approval from her, did not integrate the concept and dismissed it immediately. The power of the intervention was minimized because the husband did not keep it to himself long enough to have it affect his thinking or behavior. Apparently threatened with the growth of her husband and the change in the homeostasis of the couple, the wife later stated, "Going to that therapist is merely a waste of time."

SYSTEMIC INTERVENTIONS WITH INDIVIDUALS

While individual therapy pays attention to the intrapsychic issues of a client, it also needs to have strong systemic foundations. Intrapsychic issues manifest themselves in circular ways in relationships. "Individuals are best understood within their interrelational contexts. A comprehensive systemic view of the family focuses on the evolving relationships of the family members within their environmental, historical, developmental, and ideological contexts" (Fleuridas, Nelson, & Rosenthal, 1986, p. 113). A circular perspective emphasizes cyclical sequences of interactions.

The following suggests several systemic and circular questions in response to individually expressed thoughts and concerns. Consider the following systemic concepts and theoretical directions that could be taken by the therapist to deepen the understanding when an individual client states, "I feel very incompetent." Such a statement might be reflective of early introjected feelings.

Client: I feel very incompetent.
Therapist: That makes me sad. How long have you felt this way?
Client: For what seems to be all my life.
Therapist: How did you learn to think like this?
Client: I suppose from my father. I was never good enough. He always
    criticized me. I don't remember any encouragement.

The client's feelings might suggest a lack of differentiation from family of origin . . .

Client: I feel very incompetent.
Therapist: When do you feel incompetent the most?

Client: When I am around my father.
Therapist: Have you ever talked to him about your feelings?
Client: No. I wouldn't dare.

The feeling of incompetence might be part of a specific reciprocal interaction between spouses . . .

Client: I feel very incompetent.
Therapist: How does your spouse relate to you when you feel this way?
Client: He puts me down even more.

The client's feeling could best be understood as an automatic thought, a concept used in cognitive theory.

Client: I feel very incompetent.
Therapist: Do you think this way in every context?
Client: No.
Therapist: Then when do you think well of yourself?

By nonverbally empathizing and asking circular questions from different systemic perspectives, the therapist works toward client insight (Penn, 1982). In terms of the marital dyad, the therapist who thinks in systemic ways can make an educated guess that the statement "I feel incompetent" reflects parental criticism and inferiority which was internalized by one spouse and then projected onto the other:

Therapist: You are very hard on yourself. How does your spouse respond
and relate to your feeling of inferiority?
Client: She criticizes me all the time.

While such an intervention might initially place blame onto the spouse, the following intervention begins the steps toward true systemic understanding.

Therapist: Do you think you might "set up" your partner to criticize you?
Wife: I never thought about that.
Therapist: The pattern does seem similar to your background, so I wonder
what part you are playing in the repetition?

Systemic interventions, which seek personal responsibility, will also permit the client to examine his or her own behavior rather than undermining or criticizing an absent parent or partner.

A personal sense of power is often achieved through the ability to reflect and understand one's own functioning and responsibility in both the positive and negative aspects of a dyad. Taking personal responsibility for part of the difficulty in any relationship gives the individual an opportunity to stimulate change without waiting for the other's movement. Systems change most often when an individual understands his or her contribution to the relationship dynamics and works to alter his or her own behavior. In contrast, powerlessness is most often felt and enacted when a client is projecting all responsibility and blame onto another person.

A systemically oriented therapist practicing individual therapy will confront clients to help them become more personally insightful and self-responsible. Although the following interventions might seem harsh out of the context of therapy, a spouse frequently feels empowered when she or he senses that she or he can do something to change the current quality of the marital relationship. Personal insight and self-responsibility are the keys when the therapist confronts from a systemic perspective. Examples of interventions that ask a client to accept responsibility are:

(1) *Husband:* My wife is always critical.
   Therapist: Can you think about what you might do that leads her to criticize you? Try to answer without talking about her.

(2) *Wife:* My husband is never emotional.
   Therapist: Would you be frightened if he were?
   Do you do anything that might contribute to it being safe or unsafe for him to express his emotions?

A common problem for couples is when one or both partners is critical or judgmental. Criticism and judgment can be turned into insight by exploring what part or role the client plays in creating or maintaining the partner's behavior and how the entire pattern may relate to issues in the client's family of origin. Further suggestions for interventions that seek personal responsibility are:

• What part do you play in what you describe?
• How do you contribute to that behavior in your partner?

- What is your investment in what your partner is doing?
- Do you look for verification of those negative thoughts?
- Is your partner responding to what you are asking for?
- How is what you are describing predictable from understanding your background?

An additional benefit is that interventions that seek self-responsibility help to prevent the tendency of the therapist to become inducted into the individual client's way of thinking. For example, a woman comes to therapy complaining about what a tyrant her father has been all her life. The therapist, who has become inducted into the client's thinking over several sessions, develops a perspective that the father must be quite cruel. After several weeks, the daughter invites her father into the therapy session. Instead of meeting an aggressive, large man, as the therapist expected, the father is a diminutive, soft-spoken person who cried over the loss of his daughter. The image the daughter developed about her father when she was a child became fixed and never matured. If the therapist had asked some systemic questions such as "When your father is a 'tyrant' what do you do?" or "Have you tried to talk to him without being reactive yourself?" the persectives of the client might have been challenged in a new way. By asking the client to examine her responsibility in the parent-child relationship she might have developed a more accepting position.

INDIVIDUAL SESSIONS IN CONJOINT THERAPY

The intermingling of individual sessions with conjoint sessions can have both positive, and complicating, if not negative results. Positively, individual sessions can:

- create a closer tie of each partner to the therapist, often the result being an increased commitment to therapy.
- enrich the therapist's understanding of the family of origin and how it is related to current dynamics.
- assess the individual client's manner of relating outside the marital relationship.
- allow for a deeper psychological or psychiatric assessment without the client being self-conscious of the partner's involvement.

- establish a clearer understanding of a client's commitment to the relationship.
- allow for ventilation of intense feelings that might block the interaction in conjoint therapy.
- learn about secrets that might be blocking the progress of the marital work.

Negatively, individual sessions can:

- create difficulties with confidentiality.
- create an alignment between one partner and the therapist, possibly excluding the other partner.
- allow for one spouse to use the individual sessions as a weapon by putting the partner down.
- appear to or in fact label one partner as the "sick one."
- unwittingly split the couple as each partner begins to grow individually but apart (Berman, 1982).

When changing the structure of therapy from individual to conjoint work, the following issues should be considered. In many cases one spouse has been asking the partner to enter therapy, but the partner has refused. With a sense of desperation, the individual goes into therapy alone to attempt to make progress in the relationship. If the therapist has been systemic in approach, the partner not in therapy often realizes that the therapist is not biased against him or her. The absent partner often observes his or her spouse working on the family of origin or taking personal responsibility for his or her part of the problem. The client might say to the spouse, "The therapist really confronted me about the way I _____ with you." If the therapy is approached systemically, the nonparticipating partner might grow to understand that the therapist can be fair and balanced. Although the absent partner might have interpreted being blamed, she or he now finds that the partner in therapy is growing and taking responsibility. This fact can change the status quo of the relationship.

Including a spouse or partner into an ongoing individual therapy can be problematic. Sometimes it simply should not be done. The alignment and loyalties of the individual spouse and therapist may be too strong. If the duration of the individual therapy is over two or three months, a very positive transference might have developed. In such a transference the relationship between client and therapist can be very strong. As the individual client works out unresolved past relationships within the transferential relationship with the therapist, a level of inclusion is developed that seeks to boundary out other people, including a spouse. The longer the duration of the individual work, the greater the likelihood that a different therapist should do the couples work. (See Chapter 3 on Balanced Intervention.)

With this taken into consideration, an advantage of using the individual therapist for conjoint therapy is that the therapist already understands some of the system issues. Furthermore, due to the systemic approach in which the client was being asked to take responsibility for a portion of the marital dynamics, the nonparticipating spouse might have already gained some trust in the process of therapy and the fairness of the therapist. The following are some suggestions for including a spouse or partner after individual therapy has already begun:

1. The client who has already established a relationship with the therapist needs to understand that when the partner is added to the therapy, and the therapist establishes a balanced approach in the session, she or he might experience some loss or anger at the absence of what heretofore had been a private loyalty and relationship. Forewarning often eases the intensity of these feelings. The therapist might say, "When your partner comes to therapy, I will listen and attempt to understand both your perspectives and you might experience this as loss. Please let me know if such is the case."

2. The joining spouse or partner might participate in two or three individual sessions to join with the therapist before the conjoint sessions begin. The therapist can share with this partner some concern about possible feelings of being sided against or not being fairly understood. Again, if the new client is encouraged to share those feelings with the therapist in the session, and the therapist is balanced, they are rarely disruptive to the therapy.

3. At the commencement of the conjoint process, and at pertinent times thereafter, the therapist might verbalize all of the above with both partners present. This tends to create a commonly understood goal of balance and fairness among all parties.

CONCLUSION

In conclusion, individual sessions can be conceptualized from a systemic orientation. If such is the case, personal responsibility and insight will be sought in order that the individual might enter his or her couple system in more effective and powerful ways. While it is sometimes difficult to create couple's cases out of individual ones, it can be done if a systemic approach has been practiced consistently.

PART II

BASIC APPROACHES AND TECHNIQUES

Chapter 8

Enhancing Intimacy in Relationships

Marital and family therapists have focused primarily on eliminating pathology. Their interventions are usually designed to help resolve particular difficulties on problems such as marital conflict, poor communications, and conflicting sets of expectations. Such an emphasis is not surprising in light of the fact that theories of marital and family therapy stress pathology and symptom resolution in the same way that traditional theories of individual therapy stress pathology. Renewed interest in the *Diagnostic and Statistical Manual of Mental Disorders* (DSM-III-R) (APA, 1987) has refocused attention on pathology rather than on normalcy and health.

Most of the techniques presented in this volume will address the question of how to reduce or eliminate marital pathology. This chapter will do just the opposite. The purpose of this chapter is to present concepts and techniques that can be used to promote healthy functioning in the couple. A clinician working from a problem-solving model is only concerned with the presented problem(s). The clinician may not have a sense of how to proceed beyond symptom resolution because he or she is lacking a conceptual framework of intimacy and the skills to create higher functioning. The clinician may also lack a growth-oriented framework in which to use various techniques designed to enhance the couple.

Marital therapy is unique among the psychotherapies because it involves the treatment of a relationship defined in a very specific way in our culture. The word that captures the essence of this relationship—love—has been considered taboo in the professional literature. Marital therapy involves the treatment of a *love*(ing) relationship, yet theories of marital and family therapy rarely mention the word love. Love has been dismissed to softer disciplines such as drama, poetry, and fiction. Therapists who adhere to the scientist-practitioner model find the use of love difficult because it cannot be operationalized or measured. Researchers have found the concept of love elusive; clinicians find it troublesome because they usually think of asking only whether the partners love each other. This question is often responded to negatively at the beginning of therapy.

An exception to the clinical use of the concept of love is in the area of marital enrichment. The enrichment movement predated and subsequently merged with the human potential movement of the 1960s. Although this movement never established a large foothold in the clinical field, many psychotherapy programs were developed to promote healthier, happier, more loving relationships.

When two people are married the fact is that we are treating a type of relationship uniquely defined. Marriage is a voluntary, yet ideally permanent relationship, as opposed to family which is also permanent, yet involuntary. The basis for marriage is emotional, and the emotional attachment is defined in terms of love. Finally, marriage is the only relationship in which there exists sexual permission and expectation. This fact adds another dimension to the relationship, which in turn may become another area for relational problems.

In this chapter we will focus not only on love, but also on sex and intimacy. These concepts are inseparable, in spite of the fact that marital therapists have indirectly claimed love and intimacy as their territory and sex therapists have claimed sex as theirs. Committed couples do not split these concepts unless they are experiencing difficulties. However, clinical couples frequently split off certain aspects of their relationship. For example, a couple might split sex off so that they claim to be close without having sex, or partners might engage in an extramarital affair claiming the sexual relationship is meaningless. These couples need an explicit idea of love just as much as the clinician. Until recently, the psychological literature did not have any models of love that were clinically useful. A model now exists that is extremely useful when taken as one part of the comprehensive program which follows. This model of love consists of three components—commitment, intimacy, and passion.

THE TRIANGLE OF LOVE

In working with couples, the first step is to ask them to describe what they think comprises a loving relationship. At this point, the clinician wants a general answer in order to move to a description of the triangular

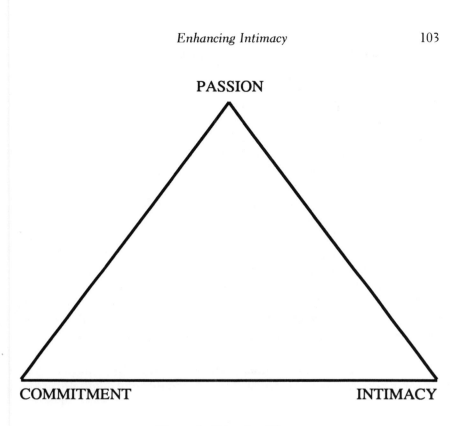

Figure 1. Triangle of Love

theory of love. After the couple have responded, the clinician begins a description by drawing a triangle with three equal sides and labels them as shown in Figure 1.

Sternberg (1986a, b) developed a triangular theory of love based on research in social psychology and personality. Love is defined as the combination of three components, and these components need to be defined for the couple. The first component is commitment. This component is cognitive or "cold." At some point in the couple's relationship a decision was made to commit to each other. They made certain societally sanctioned promises to each other regarding exclusivity.

Commitment

The first issue to discuss with the couple is their definition of commitment. Do they share the same definition? Are they committed, uncommitted, ambivalent, or unequally committed? We believe one of the most important factors in the outcome of marital therapy is commitment. When a couple come for therapy and they both say they are equally committed to the marriage, we usually see the couple resolve their problems. The couple can also be congratulated for maintaining their commitment to each other as people, in spite of the fact that each may be doing things the other does not like.

When the couple are ambivalent, have unequal commitment, or are lacking in commitment, an open discussion needs to take place so that each partner's thoughts and feelings are understood. The purpose of this technique is to obtain a commitment to treatment long enough to explore the relationship. This will allow the couple to see whether marital functioning can be restored or whether there should be a separation. When couples end therapy prematurely, they frequently continue to go "back and forth" and never have an opportunity to thoroughly understand the part each played in the marriage not working out. In short, when couples cannot commit to each other, they need to make a commitment to the therapeutic process.

In cases where the commitment is weak or one partner is ambivalent about continuing the relationship, a number of different approaches may be taken to help increase commitment. These approaches are based on social-psychological research. Harold Kelley (1983) reviewed major findings related to the process of commitment, that is, those intra- and interpersonal processes that help to establish and to sustain stability. One way to sustain commitment is to improve the reward-cost balance in the relationship. In clinical terms, two tactics may be taken with the client. The first is to ask the partner to think back to what has been rewarding about the relationship.

As the partner begins to remember these positive interactions, it helps to remind the person of past rewards. The partner is next asked if those rewards could be reinstated, would she or he be willing to continue in the relationship. The second tactic is future-oriented. The partner is asked to think about what she or he would need to feel happy or satisfied in the relationship. The person's partner is asked whether he or she would be able to meet these needs. The less committed partner may be willing to sustain the relationship in the hope of receiving future rewards. The therapy would then involve working towards the fulfillment of the needs stated at this point.

Another factor related to commitment is that of irretrievable investments. In any relationship of significant duration the partners have made intangible investments that will be lost if the relationship ends. It is useful to talk about these investments. The therapist might ask, "What kinds of investments have you already made in this relationship?" The most useful investments are those that tap into what the partner has contributed emotionally.

A third factor in commitment deals with the understanding that occurs between partners. Over time partners develop a sense of mutual understanding. A sense of "we-ness." They have an identity as a couple. They know their roles, develop a history together, and create their own private language. All these attributes would be lost if the relationship ends, and the process would have to occur again in any new relationship. Having the partner think about the value of this understanding and its replacement can further promote commitment.

A final factor that has clinical relevance is that of considering the attractiveness of alternative relationships. Any time a partner considers leaving one relationship, there is always the thought of whether there will be another to replace it. One way to increase commitment to the process of therapy, as well as the relationship, is to discuss the need for understanding what happened in the current relationship in terms of that person's contribution to the problems. The therapist may point out that ending a relationship without this understanding may result in a repetition of the same problem in the next relationship. By suggesting that the problem can be carried over into the next relationship, it is obvious that the attractiveness of the next relationship is being reduced. In addition, leaving a relationship with ambivalent feelings also may result in indecision and a pattern of moving in and out of the current problematic relationship. If the clinician can engage the ambivalent partner in treatment for an extended period of time, the prognosis for the couple is very favorable. Commitment should not be underestimated as a variable in the treatment process. A high degree of commitment to the process is highly correlated with a successful outcome.

Intimacy

The second component of the triangle is intimacy. More has been written about intimacy than about the other two components (Sloan & L'Abate, 1985). Sternberg (1986) refers to intimacy as the sense of feeling close, connected, or bonded, having a sense of welfare for the other, wanting happiness for the other, regarding the other highly, being able to count on the other in times of need, experiencing mutual understanding, sharing oneself and other possessions, talking intimately, giving emotional support, valuing the other, and finding the other person predictable (trustworthy). After mentioning a few words to describe intimacy, the clinician should point out that every couple and individual has his or her own definitions of intimacy, and ask each partner to briefly define intimacy with the idea that this question will be discussed later in much more depth.

Passion

The third component of the love triangle is passion. Passion has been described as romance, sex, physical affection, affiliation, nurturance, and the longing to be with the other person. Once again the technique is to describe this term briefly and then ask about the partners' definitions.

Clinical Application of the Triangle

The triangle serves as the structure for much of the subsequent work. It is used initially to explore commitment and for purposes of assessing where the love relationship is lacking. In the process of describing the triangle, the clinician wants to ask five diagnostic questions. These questions may be posed directly or indirectly depending on the openness and sophistication of the couple and the style of the therapist.

1. The first question is whether both partners desire all three components. There are obvious cases in which one partner may deny any commitment (e.g., "I want a divorce") or deny having any sexual interest (passion) in the other (e.g., inhibited sexual desire). In less obvious cases, one partner may say he or she wants a particular component but fails to have any grasp of what that component involves. A common case is the husband who wants intimacy but equates intimacy to such things as sex, a backrub, or helping in his business.

2. The second question is whether each partner wants the same level of intensity for each component. The partners should be asked whether they believe they desire the same level of intensity in these three areas or whether they experience discrepancies. The clinician should note whether one or more areas is given too little or too

much emphasis. For example, a couple might emphasize how great sex (passion) is to the exclusion of the other areas. When there are discrepancies, the therapist needs to guide the couple toward developing an agreed upon level.

3. The third question is what prevents the identification and expression of these three components? Each partner should be able to: (a) identify and define the components, and (b) express each component openly and freely. For many couples there may be an *intellectual* identification and definition of a component without the concomitant ability to express the component emotionally or behaviorally. The therapist should ask the partners to think directly about what prevents him or her from being able to express certain feelings. The clinician should carefully examine the question from the perspective of the *Intersystem Model* described in the Introduction and fears of intimacy to be discussed later in this chapter.

4. The fourth question is whether each partner has a realistic perception of what love involves. Some partners think of loving relationships in ways that are highly distorted and unrealistic. As mentioned earlier, the clinician should ascertain whether the three components are given too much or too little emphasis. At this point, it is useful to listen for some of the common myths of marriage such as, "If she or he really loved me, she or he would automatically know what I want."

5. The fifth question is whether each partner has a realistic perception of what she or he can offer or has been able to offer. As the couple talk about the three areas, it will become apparent whether an individual is able to actually deliver on what is being stated. The partner's feedback and the way in which the partners interact provide information about their limitations.

Teaching the model of love and asking these five diagnostic/therapeutic questions set the stage for the task of promoting intimacy in the couple. The next step involves asking the couple to identify the specific components of intimacy and then to think about what behaviors constitute an intimate relationship. In addition to the list generated by the couple, we add additional ideas from L'Abate's (1977) work on intimacy and marital enrichment.

In addition to Sternberg's model of love, Zick Rubin (1973) conducted an empirical study in which love was found to have four major components. These components are (1) needing (the desire to be with and cared for by the other); (2) caring (wanting to help the other); (3) trusting (exchanging confidences); and (4) tolerance (overlooking the other person's faults). Rubin also found that partners did not desire these four components in the same degree. In fact, in some relationships low correlations existed between some components. These components can all be incorporated in Sternberg's (1986) model under the heading of intimacy.

The component of tolerance is one that should be more carefully considered here because it is not mentioned elsewhere in this chapter. Successful couples learn where each other's faults and perceived weaknesses lie. Of necessity, they need to find ways to work around these areas rather than continue to press or nag each other for perfection. The perspective of a loving couple needs to be on the positives and not the negatives. Part of the process of marital therapy is learning to accept those aspects of the partner that this person does not desire to change nor need to change in order to improve the overall level of marital satisfaction.

Our technique then involves reviewing the seven components of intimacy listed below, followed by how the couple will move from a conceptual level to a behavioral level. The clinician reviews these items and then starts at the top of the list to allow the couple to discuss each one in order. The couple decide whether they like the ideas that have been generated and how to implement the ideas. The couple then start with a new set of ideas or attitudes about what constitutes intimacy. Once they agree to these ideas mutually, the next step is behavioral. They are asked to describe exactly what they are willing to do to carry out the idea. In the following sessions the therapist asks about the behavioral progress. In addition, an affective component is added by asking that the partners comment on how they feel when they receive some of the intimacy behaviors. In the session they are also asked to discuss their feelings toward their partner in light of the behavioral changes.

Components of Intimacy

The components L'Abate (1977) has identified are:

1. SEEING THE GOOD

Each partner should be able to see the good both in self as well as in the other. Each should be able to say what is good in self and express what he or she likes about the other. The behavioral implementation could involve statements of affirmation, appreciation, and affection. We refer to this triad as the three A's and suggest couples practice it daily. Statements of *affirmation* are "I like you" in nature. These statements affirm the value of the other person. For example, saying "I'm glad I'm married to you" or "I like being with you" refer to the love for the other person. Statements of *appreciation* deal with what the other person does. When the other person does something that is liked, it should be verbally noted. The third A is *affection*. Touching, holding, kissing, and making verbal statements of affection are also important.

2. Caring

A caring attitude toward oneself and the other is important. Caring can be shown in many ways as defined by the couple. Being concerned with the other's welfare, life, and feelings on a consistent and dependable basis is essential. It is important that the person showing the caring give to the other what she or he also defines as being cared for.

3. Protectiveness

A couple is a social system embedded within other social systems. Many forces impinge on the couple such as work, in-laws, and children. The couple must protect the integrity of their relationship by drawing boundaries around it. They must also give each other the time required to be a couple.

4. Enjoyment

Enjoyment refers to giving pleasure to oneself and sharing pleasure with one's partner. In our society many people have been taught that pleasure is not a goal in itself nor even desirable. These individuals have been trained to believe that performance is all important. The emphasis is placed on doing, achieving, and competition. This need to perform in order to win approval and love needs to be examined and a healthy attitude fostered to replace it. This new attitude should involve learning to give pleasure and enjoyment to oneself in order to share it with the partner. Couples can be encouraged to negotiate activities they both enjoy just for the sake of pleasure. Part of this process also requires that each partner accept some responsibility for initiating enjoyable activities.

5. RESPONSIBILITY

When problems emerge in a relationship there is a tendency to deny personal responsibility by externalizing blame onto one's partner. In an intimate relationship each partner must take responsibility for his or her part in the relationship not working. Healthy interdependence rests on personal responsibility, not on one partner taking all the blame or on one partner giving all the blame.

6. SHARING HURT

Unhealthy relationships are often characterized by an intense level of anger. In such cases the only feeling expressed or in evidence seems to be anger. In these relationships, all the underlying feelings have been buried by the anger. These buried feelings may include hurt, depression, resentment, frustration, guilt, remorse, and so on. Hurt is especially prone to be buried because it is seen as a weakness. When anger is used to cover over other feelings, the expression and resolution of the underlying problem(s) are impossible, rendering each partner powerless. Learning to share hurt rather than burying it is critical in promoting understanding and empathy. The therapist may ask the partners to consider all the feelings felt, but not expressed, and then facilitate the expression of the underlying feelings in the session, focusing on hurt.

7. FORGIVENESS

In an intimate relationship partners will from time to time act in ways that are hurtful. If these acts are not or cannot be forgiven, a state of resentment is established which erodes the relationship. Several questions are useful to facilitate forgiveness. Forgiveness is not achieved by making a simple apology. It is achieved through an understanding of self and other. First, the person who committed the hurtful act should question him- or herself about motivations. This self-inquiry is most salient when hurting the other is part of a pattern. Second, the partners must understand each other. The person who was hurt needs to be validated for feeling hurt and the partner who did the hurting needs to be understood in terms of his or her motivations and intents. The intent should ultimately be that of not wanting to hurt the other.

Once again, the review of these components is best accomplished over a number of sessions. The ideas are developed and then techniques to implement them discussed. Each week the therapist should check in to see how progress is going on those items discussed.

One final note on intimacy has to do with how couples conceptualize closeness. Many couples simply equate intimacy with physical closeness. A technique to help make this expectation explicit is to ask them to draw two circles to show closeness, each circle representing self. The partners are told to draw two circles representing how they see themselves now and two circles representing how they should ideally like to be. The circles can then be used to facilitate a discussion in which the clinician would point out that intimacy is a balance between closeness and distance and that couples need to negotiate these two ideas in some practical way. The idea of negotiating distance is new to many couples. Usually they ask for distance indirectly or by creating a fight. In one young couple the assumption was that all free time would be spent together. Each partner believed the other expected them to give up any interest that might take them away from the relationship. Once they realized how counterproductive this idea was, they were able to schedule time for personal interests and be in the house together without feeling compelled to be together.

FEARS OF INTIMACY

Many couples experience difficulty in becoming more intimate, although they have some awareness of what it means and what they want. When this problem is apparent from the outset, the following technique should be used *first*. In addition, if the problem appears in the process of working through developing greater intimacy, work should be halted and the Intimacy—Fear Awareness technique used.

The technique involves making the implicit, and sometimes unconscious, fears of intimacy explicit. It is often helpful to normalize these fears by noting how some of them are found in most everyone. The couple would then be asked to consider what fears each brought to the relationship. It is essential to keep the discussion framed in terms of fear. A slow and careful therapeutic examination will usually uncover one or more fears that can then be worked through.

The clinician may need to supply some ideas based on observations made of the couple and their individual dynamics, including family-of-origin information. A number of the common fears are historically based in the family of origin. The following list is helpful for the clinician to keep in mind. This list is not exhaustive. It represents some of the most common fears.

Fears of Dependency

This fear is found in partners who believe it is absolutely essential to be emotionally self-sufficient, insulated, and independent. In extreme cases, the partner exhibits counterdependency or the need to constantly remain aloof from the other as if to say she or he does not need the other at all but finds the partner a financial or social convenience. This pattern can be found in marriages which Sager and Hunt (1979) have called parallel. These couples do not rely on each other to fulfill their emotional needs. The marriage is characterized by emotional distance, with each leading separate lives.

The fear of dependence often stems from early parental influence. Parents, usually fathers, share the importance of being able to stand alone in the world without having to rely on anyone. During childhood, children who grow up to fear dependence are pushed to be on their own with little, if any, guidance or support from the parent. When these children do need help they are told they are weak or that they should be able to do it alone. This fear appears in men much more often than in women and is passed from father to son.

> To illustrate this pattern, one 40-year-old man stated he could never ask his wife for anything. He believed to ask her for something meant he was weak and "a nothing." As a child, this man had been physically punished and ridiculed whenever he showed any emotional weakness such as crying, and he was ridiculed as being a baby when he expressed needs of his own. He had internalized his father's expressed emotions so strongly that he actually felt he would die should he express his needs. Although he realized this feeling was irrational, he could not stop this feeling on his own. It was based on the belief that only the strong have the will to survive.

Fear of Feelings

Expressing intimacy involves sharing a feeling with another person. Some partners have learned to fear their feelings. The feelings they fear are not specific ones such as the fear of hurt, rejection, and abandonment, but a general fear of all feelings. It is true this general fear might be related to fear of specific feelings originally. Unfortunately, the specific fear has generalized to include expressing any feeling.

Partners who have obsessive-compulsive personality structure use their defenses to avoid feelings, and indeed these individuals seem devoid of feeling. They hide behind rationality, intellectualization, and a rigid sense of what they believe to be right. Satir (1967) referred to these types of partners as computers because of their mechanical non-feeling approach to others. Computers think rather than feel, think rather than act, and stay detached from others in order to avoid having their own feelings touched. Being so devoid of an emotional life of their own they sometimes enter into a relationship with a histrionic partner, and on the surface they act as if the other partner were sick or crazy, but unconsciously they derive some gratification. The feelings obsessive-compulsive partners find uncomfortable may be projected onto their partner so that they can then deal with the feeling in the other and not in self.

Individuals reared in families where feelings were out of control may also learn to avoid their own feelings. In situations where child abuse or alcoholism was prevalent or if a parent suffered from depression, a manic-depressive reaction, or was emotionally unpredictable, the child might fear being overwhelmed by feelings and losing control or going crazy. In these partners' minds the idea of feeling is synonymous with craziness. The same dynamic may also occur in individuals who have suffered from long-term depression. In several of our cases, men with long untreated depressions felt that allowing any feeling is the same as inviting an occurrence of depression.

A final pattern of fear occurs in those individuals who were emotionally discounted and/or told how to feel by their parents. Being emotionally discounted means the parents would ignore, criticize, or punish the child for having a feeling. Because emotional discounting is a verbal process and less severe than other types of abuse, it is often overlooked. However, repeated emotional discounting can have several long-term effects. Adults we have treated believe their partners will discount them should they attempt to express a feeling. They learn to ignore, minimize, and ratio-nalize their feelings. The pattern is further complicated because these clients do not share their feelings with the therapist, giving the impression that everything is satisfactory. The therapist must learn to listen for what is not expressed as much as to what is expressed.

Fear of Anger

The fear of anger may manifest in two ways. First, partners may fear the anger they have toward others. They may fear that getting too close to another person may elicit or release this hostility, aggression, anger, and/or rage. Individuals with this fear keep their distance from others. They realize anger is inevitable in a close relationship so they rationalize that the only way to avoid it is to not have a close relationship. Several types of familial environments may create this type of fear in an individual. In one type of family the child may be parentified. Parentified children are asked to assume responsibility far beyond their capacity. They must act like pseudoadults often cast in the role of taking care of a parent. The loss of the child's sense of security, the excessive demands, and the pent-up feeling of anger that is not allowed to be expressed builds up over time. Many partners who were parentified carry deeply buried resentment and anger that is displaced onto their current partner.

Another family situation that generates fear of anger is one in which anger pervaded the system. Child and/or spouse abuse may have taken place. The child witnesses how anger got out of control and how members of the family got hurt. In an effort to never repeat this pattern, the adult partner tries to suppress anger. The partner believes anger can only have destructive consequences, as a result of the model set by the parents. The opposite type of family environment can have the same effect. In these families the parents are reported to have never been angry or in conflict. The parents implicitly transmit the message that anger is bad, unacceptable, destructive, and so on. In many of these families children are told directly it is not nice to be angry or that something is wrong with them if they feel anger.

In other cases, partners simply may not have the skills to deal with anger. As a result, angry feelings never get resolved and build up over a period of time. The feeling may escalate to the point of violence, scaring themselves and their partner so much they vow never to be angry again. Of course, this effort is doomed to fail, but the fear still remains.

The other major manifestation of this fear is that of being the recipient of angry feelings. These individuals are very fearful that their partners will become angry with them. They will go to great lengths to placate the partner in order to avoid anger. Just as in the above case where these persons fear their own anger, these individuals may have been reared in families where anger was expressed too much or too little. Most commonly they were reared in families where the anger was explosively and unpredictably expressed. Children of alcoholics come to realize that the alcoholic's anger is unpredictable, unwarranted, and intended as destructive. These childen then live in a state of constant fear waiting for something bad to happen to them or to another family member.

Fear of Losing Control or Being Controlled

This fear has two levels of meaning. On the surface, it refers to the feeling that getting too intimate will result in a loss of control in one's life. This partner believes the other person will begin to take over and run his or her life. Essentially, it is a regressive feeling of being a child again with the other partner assuming a parental role. This feeling parallels what happened in the person's family of origin. The parents were overcontrolling, did not promote competency and maturity, and may have actually set the child up to fail by pushing them into tasks beyond his or her capabilities and then withholding guidance and support.

At a deeper intrapsychic level, losing control means feeling engulfed by the partner. Engulfment refers to losing oneself in a relationship; the person's tenuous sense of self-identity gets lost. These individuals are poorly differentiated, and they have a poorly defined sense of self. Paradoxically, they search out others to help them complete their sense of self, but then they need to recoil from the relationship to preserve the sense of self they already possess. They tend to move back and forth searching for a balance. These individuals must search out their own identity and actively seek others who will support them and respect individual boundaries.

Fear of Exposure

Early on in a relationship, partners only expose what they choose to expose. The partners only see the façade. As the relationship develops the couple become closer and more self-disclosing.

The level of self-disclosure zig-zags to deeper levels with partners taking turns risking more disclosure as trust builds. The question for every partner early on is, "How much to disclose and when?" However, self-disclosure may stop at a surface level out of the fear that exposing oneself will be too painful. A partner with a low sense of self-worth or self-esteem will not want his or her partner to know. She or he will pretend to feel good about him- or herself. For these partners, the family did not provide sufficient development of self-worth. The parents may have been critical, demanding, or never satisfied with their child's performance.

In many of these families, the love for the child was contingent on performance and not the person. Contingent love teaches the child to value only doing well and not self. The child learns she or he is loved only when things are going well. If a problem or unpleasant feeling is expressed, the child immediately loses sight of the fact that love can be a constant in the relationship. In order to protect themselves from feeling unloved, they would not consider telling their partner how they feel, if it were negative, and would expect their partner to do likewise. The basic assumption of these individuals is that if you really knew me, you would not like or love me (because I do not really like or love myself).

Fear of Abandonment/Rejection

The more a partner emotionally invests in a relationship, the greater the hurt is experienced should the relationship end. Partners who have been hurt in the past because others have rejected/abandoned them are sensitive to getting too close too soon or to getting close at all. In more serious cases, the partner has been traumatically rejected or abandoned. This situation might have occurred through death, divorce, or desertion of a parent. Children who have lost a parent and have not been aided in working through the loss sometimes carry a fear of abandonment to all subsequent relationships. Children who learn they were adopted may also carry a deep sense of rejection and abandonment. In other cases, the family of origin did not contribute to the fear. The fear may have evolved through adult relationships that were extraordinarily hurtful.

In some cases, we have seen partners suddenly abandoned just prior to a wedding without any explanation or further contact with the person. In one case, a person's partner had been killed in an airline accident and, simultaneously, it was discovered that the partner was having an affair. These events left the partner with a deep sense of loss, rejection, and hurt. In a case like this, never getting close to another person is seen as a way to protect oneself from ever having to relive such a painful trauma.

CONCLUSION

A number of concepts and techniques have been reviewed in this chapter. The clinician should use them flexibly, creatively, and according to the type of couple. There is no formula for developing intimacy. The ideas in this chapter constitute a blueprint—the couple provide the bricks, mortar, and sweat.

Chapter 9

Reframing

Reframing is the most generically used strategy in the systems therapies as well as psychotherapy in general. It is fundamental for psychotherapy because it helps the client change perspective, thereby facilitating change in attitude and behavior. Systems therapists have referred to this concept by a variety of terms: relabeling (Haley, 1973; Minuchin, 1974); reframing (Watzlawick, Weakland, & Fisch, 1974); content reframing (Bandler & Grinder, 1982); redefinition (Andolfi, 1979); seeing the good (L'Abate, 1975); positive connotation (Palazzoli, Boscolo, Cecchin, & Prata, 1978); ascribing noble intention (Stanton, Todd, & Associates, 1982); non-blaming (Alexander & Parsons, 1982); and context markers (Bateson, 1979; L'Abate, Ganahl, & Hansen, 1986; Viaro, 1980).

Watzlawick and colleagues (1974) were among the first to discuss the central role of reframing in therapy. They defined reframing as changing the conceptual and/or emotional meaning attributed to a situation and said that the behavior reframed is the behavior that has been defined or framed by the client as being symptomatic.

A reframing statement is quite different from an interpretation. For example, interpretation carries some truth value and the therapist actually believes the statement represents some aspect of reality. On the other hand, reframing statements are not intended to have the same validity. The theory of truth that is used by the therapist in reframing is pragmatic. In the pragmatic theory of truth, that which works is considered true (James, 1907). The therapist is attempting to construct a view of reality that is more conducive for change to occur, rather than replace the client's faulty world view with one that is correct (Kelly, 1955). Tennen, Eron, and Rohrbaugh (1985) have stated:

> Adaptive functioning does not require being in touch with reality
> and having an accurate view of the world. Rather, *any* world view
> that interdicts problem sequences is considered in planning inter-
> ventions. This position is nested not only in "functional theory,"

118

but in growing empirical literature pointing to the healing effects of illusion (Lazarus, 1983; Taylor, 1983). Adaptive functioning has been associated with denial (Lazarus, 1983), the illusion of control (Alloy & Abramson, 1979; Tiger, 1979) and the misperception of one's success and its causes (Greenwald, 1980; Miller & Ross, 1975). High self-esteem (Tennen & Herzberger, submitted for publication; Tennen et al., submitted for publication), lack of depression (Lewinsohn et al., 1980; Abramson & Alloy, 1981) and better adjustment to illness and injury (Bulman & Wortman, 1977; Taylor, 1983; Tennen et al., in press) have been associated with *non-verdical* and illogical perceptions and beliefs. The shift from psyche to system and from reality testing to useful illusions may represent the most significant contributions of the strategic therapist in his/her use of paradox. (pp. 199–200)

In order to effectively reframe the symptom, the therapist must first join with the client system and understand the symptom. These tasks occur during assessment.

Every system of therapy attempts to change the meaning of the problem or symptom in some fashion (Weeks, 1977, 1990). The use of reframing in the literature usually has two meanings (Weeks & L'Abate, 1982). One is to change the way in which a symptom is defined in terms of some polarization such as good versus bad, crazy versus sane. This use of reframing stems from the various models of psychotherapy. Clients frequently attribute bad intent to their behavior. In couples, this attributional process leads one to the moral perspective that they are okay and the other is bad. Reframing can be used to change the meaning attributed to the problem. For example, couples usually believe their fights are exclusively negative behaviors. The fights have been framed as destructive, negative, and so on and seen as representing negative intent. In reframing the fighting behavior, the therapist wants to change the meaning attributed from bad to good. The therapist can say, for example,

The two of you must care a great deal about each other and yourselves, because you invest so much of your energy in fighting. Couples who don't care or are indifferent don't fight. Your fighting shows there is something worth fighting for in spite of the fact that you may end up appearing to fight against each other.

The second use of reframing is to move the focus from the individual to the system. When couples or families present with problems, there is usually a symptom bearer (identified patient) who is carrying the problem for the rest of the family. The other member(s) do not see the connection between what they do and the behavior of the "sick" one. In couples, the "healthy" spouse externalizes and/or denies any responsibility for the problem. The attributional strategy in the couple is linear, not circular. One of the therapists tasks is to get them to see how the problem stems from their interaction and/or relationship. Reframing is the method whereby the therapist can move the couple from a linear attributional strategy to an interactional or circular attributional strategy.

In other words, when couples present in therapy, there is often an overt or covert belief that the other partner is wrong, sick, crazy, and so on. Thus, it is the other partner's place to change. The symptom presented is usually seen as "belonging" to just one partner and not a result of the partners' interaction. The therapist must find a way to get the couple to see the problem systemically. Unless and until they see the problem as shared or bilateral, couples therapy is impossible.

The two types of reframing described above are usually combined in a statement given to the couple. Palazzoli and coauthors (1978) called this technique positive connotation. The symptom is given a positive meaning and all the members of the system are linked together. Reframing changes the definition of the relationship, changes the meaning of the behavior by altering or disrupting the interpretative framework, and disrupts one's ability to predict another's behavior. It also puts the participants on the same level. One goal of the reframe is to prescribe a shared meaning in the relationship (e.g., "fighting means you care"). It also increases interdependence by suggesting they both want the same goal for the relationship.

Finally, one of the most significant effects is to change the attributions from linear to circular and from negative to positive. If the reframe is successful and the couple believe they both deserve the same thing, then they must ask themselves if there aren't better ways to achieve it than to engage in the same endless game. The result should be new efforts to change the other's impressions of self by changing one's behavior.

The art of reframing has been poorly described in the literature. Most literature describes the reasons for and content, but not the process involved in creating new frames. Weeks and L'Abate (1982) reviewed the literature and gave numerous examples throughout their text. Many of these examples were couple focused. In addition, Protinsky and Quinn (1981, p. 139) have developed a few standard reframes to deal with common couple and family dynamics. In one of their cases, a husband became suicidal after the last child graduated from high school and went to college. His wife had been overinvolved with rearing the children and felt a profound sense of loss. The couple were given the following reframe:

> The team is very impressed with the great lengths that Joe has gone to in order to protect his wife from her feeling of loneliness. It was Joe's intuitive belief that Mary could not survive the emptiness she felt when John graduated and left home. Thus, Joe acted in helpless ways so that Mary might fill her emptiness. This is a highly caring act on Joe's part. However, it is the team's belief that Mary does not need Joe to rescue her from loneliness in the way that he has chosen. The team perceives many hidden strengths to Joe; it is the team's belief that he will continue to act in his present protective way.

L'Abate and Samples (1983, p. 38) developed an invariable reframe for couples with intimacy problems. They used the following statement:

> Dear _____ and _____:
> After working with you for so long, I am fairly convinced that you need to defeat each other to avoid getting too close. Intimacy can be a very scary and dangerous condition, and I can understand how it affects you in that way. For some people, intimacy means loss of control, loss of mind, loss of self, loss of strength, and in some cases, loss of life.

Weeks and L'Abate (1982) and Jessee and L'Abate (1985) also developed a paradoxical approach to treating depression that included reframing depression in the context of the relationship. Jessee and L'Abate (1985, p. 1139) used the following reframe in one case:

> I think you are to be congratulated for being depressed to help your husband. It is obvious that you have become depressed in an attempt to take his mind off being unemployed. I cannot think of

anything else you could have done that would have demonstrated your caring and loyalty to him so convincingly.

While examples are very helpful, the therapist also needs to know the process involved in developing a reframe. Only one article in the literature focuses on this issue exclusively (Jones, 1986). Jones briefly touched on the importance of joining, using the client's language, and asking focused questions. All of these elements are essential in reframing. Reframing is not something the therapist does *to* the couple. In other words, the therapist cannot just offer up a reframe and expect it to be accepted.

The first step in reframing is for the therapist to develop an idea or ideas about what kind of reframe would be helpful in facilitating change. As stated earlier, for systemic change to occur there must be a systemic definition of the problem by the couple. The therapist must think ahead and then gently guide the couple toward a new definition of the problem. The therapist cannot guide the couple unless he or she has joined with them. To join means to be seen as an ally of each and both simultaneously.

Understanding each partner's perspective and the couple's common goals helps to achieve joining. The therapist can note the couple's language and use similar language. The therapist's definition of the problem and the couple's definition of the problem start out incongruent. The goal is to bring the couple in greater congruence with the therapist. The key way in which this task is completed is by slowly weaving together a series of questions that gets the couple to change their perceptions. The questions may be designed to elicit new information, to punctuate the information in a different way, or to change the meaning given to certain facts. The couple may actually articulate a new frame as a result of considering these questions. If not, when they are sufficiently "primed," the therapist may offer the reframe. If the process has been carefully completed, the reframe will take root; if not, it will be rejected sooner or later. Some couples are ready to accept a reframe with little cultivation. Others require the careful process described above. A case helps illustrate the points made above.

A couple in their mid-30s presented with a variety of problems. The major problem was that they had been dating for several years but had not been able to decide whether to marry. One of the problems that was revealed later in therapy was Ann's insomnia. Insomnia has always been conceptualized as an individual problem in the clinical literature (Ascher, Bowers, & Schotte, 1985). Ann had tried a number of remedies to eliminate her insomnia but none had worked. In fact, she failed to mention this problem early on in treatment because she had given up on believing there was any help. It was her partner, Jeff, who mentioned it. Ann saw her insomnia as an individual problem and Jeff agreed. Neither one saw any connection between her problem and their relationship problems.

The goal of the reframe for her insomnia was to give it a positive meaning for her relationship and to help them see how the insomnia was an interactional phenomenon. After careful questioning about how the couple managed conflict, the therapist suggested that Ann's insomnia served several very useful functions for their relationship. The most important function it served was to keep Ann from showing anger. A person who does not sleep does not have the energy to get angry, and her inability to become angry seemed to protect the relationship because Jeff, who always equated anger with rejection, could not deal with an angry partner. Rejection was a central theme in Jeff's history, as he felt both his parents had rejected him as a child.

The reframing statement can be briefly summarized as follows: The insomnia protects your relationship by keeping you, Ann, from getting angry with Jeff. Jeff would see your anger as rejection and leave.

This reframe can be analyzed as follows:

INTRAPSYCHIC COMPONENTS	INTERACTIONAL COMPONENTS
1. *Definition*	1. *Congruence*
The insomnia is redefined as protective for both partners. In a more general sense, the partners are defined as being in a relationship characterized by protection. They must now ask, "Are there better ways to be protective?"	Ann attempted to control her anger through insomnia in order to protect Jeff in the relationship. Jeff had sent her messages that he could not tolerate anger. Hence, they were in an incongruent relationship regarding the expression of anger. The reframe made this incongruence explicit, showed how they both participate in her symptom, and allowed them to share a common goal of protection.

2. *Interpretation*

The change in definition changes how the symptom and relationship are interrelated. They will now attribute positive meaning to the symptom.

3. *Prediction*

Ann can no longer predict that she will experience greater loss of sleep when angry. This connection had been unconscious. Jeff can no longer predict how Ann will deal with her anger or how he will deal with his sense of rejection. In fact, he requested that she let him know when she was angry, even if it was bad for him.

2. *Interdependence*

By showing how they both satisfy unconscious needs in the other, the level of interdependence is increased.

3. *Attribution and Impression Management*

The linear attribution strategy was disrupted. They both attributed a positive meaning to the symptom and to the other's intent. This in turn lead *them* to invite the other to try something different. She was asked to express her anger and he was asked to express his sense of rejection more directly.

The use of reframing in psychotherapy and marital therapy deserves considerable attention. The reader who wishes to gain a greater understanding can consult several recent reviews: Jones (1986); L'Abate, Ganahl, and Hansen (1986); Weeks (1977); and Weeks and L'Abate (1982).

In summary, reframing the symptoms has multiple effects. The most important effects in systems therapy are to change the linear attributional strategy of the couple to a circular attributional strategy and to change the attribution of meaning given the symptom to one that is positive. Positive in this case actually refers to some aspect of the relationship that helps the couple bond. The positive dynamic (e.g., protection) helps to create greater congruence by defining something that both desire. Once both partners see how they participate in the symptom, they are ready to work cooperatively rather than competitively. Additionally, by attributing positive intention(s), each partner is more open to try different strategies in dealing with the other—which means each partner must change.

CONCLUSION

Although reframing is an essential part of therapy, it is usually not sufficient to bring about change by itself. Weeks and L'Abate (1982) have presented cases where reframing was enough to effect change, but these are the exceptions. Reframing sets the stage for the second phase of therapy, prescriptive in nature.

Unless the therapist pays careful attention to the first therapeutic stage, it may be difficult or impossible to proceed. A problem that is defined by the couple in a fixed, immutable way, will be resistant to change. The clinician begins the therapeutic process by redefining the problem, even if only slightly altering meaning at first. In traditional individual therapies, problems are often redefined as having underlying origins outside the client's awareness and control. This type of redefinition moves the client away from the originally defined problem to another issue. Another common type of redefinition is to move from content to process.

In this chapter, we have stressed the concepts of moving from negative to positive frames and from individual to systemic frames. Many other frames are possible to co-construct with clients. These two are probably the most common and useful for the couples therapist. The remainder of this volume describes basic prescriptions that may be used with couples.

Chapter 10

Communication Techniques

Techniques to improve a couple's communication cut across all other techniques in this book. The sine qua non of couples therapy is communication training whether it's conducted explicitly or implicitly. Because communication is the foundation for all therapeutic work, it is a transtheoretical concept. Communication does not belong to one approach in therapy. It is part of all therapeutic approaches and constitutes an approach in and of itself. The purpose of this chapter is to present a number of communication techniques that can be used as part of strict or exclusive communications work with a couple or as part of an integrated approach, for example, communication training blended with contracting. Much of the work that has been reviewed on communication in couples shows it is psychoeducational (L'Abate & McHenry, 1983). In other words, couples require an individualized educational training or coaching process to help eliminate deficits and to create more effective means by which to communicate.

Because the purpose of this chapter is to describe techniques of communication enhancement and not theories of communication, only a basic schema of couples' communication will be presented to help guide the clinician. This schema will help the clinician facilitate communication of a kind that is helpful to couples rather than to individuals. It was developed by Bernal and Barker (1979) in an effort to draw together different theories of communication. Part of what this theory addresses is linear versus circular and content versus process communication.

Communication that is linear in nature reflects cause-effect thinking and is other- (outside of self) focused. When a partner is engaging in this type of communication, she or he does not talk about or disclose self, or he or she talks about self as simply reacting to others. Circular communication reflects a more mature, differentiated, and abstract form of thinking. At this level, partners can talk about their reciprocal, interlocking patterns of relating. For example, a husband might say he is angry over the tone in his wife's voice. She could clarify the meaning of her tone once she has this information and add that her tone was in response to his withdrawal. This couple can see how they each affect and are affected by the other. Patterns of communication begin to become clear to them through this type of discussion.

Content-oriented communication deals with just the specific content issue at hand for a couple. In content communication the couple can only think about *what* they are thinking and not about *how* they are thinking. Process communication is more mature, differentiated, and abstract. Partners can step outside themselves in order to become their own observers. They can talk about how they are talking (metacommunicate) and how they need to change dysfunctional patterns in their communication.

A couples therapist needs to facilitate moving from linear to circular and from content to process communication in order to promote healthy communication. Unfortunately, there are not any specific techniques to accomplish this goal. This process unfolds during the therapeutic interactions as the therapist points out these different communications, asks different questions, directs communication in different ways, and models these concepts. Bernal and Barker's schema may also be used psychoeducationally. It can be taught to couples so they can begin to analyze their own level of communication. There are five levels of communication in this system. These are organized from the least mature and helpful to the most mature and helpful. They could be described in the following ways:

1. *Objects:* The couple focus on issues outside of self exclusively, e.g., money, sex, in-laws. Issues related to self and the relationship are objectified and concretized, e.g., an attorney is upset that he lost a case. He tells his wife he "feels bad" and then describes the events of the case in detail. He fails to talk about himself and ends up telling her a boring story.

2. *Individual:* Each partner focuses on the other as the cause for his or her behavior. Responsibility for one's actions is disowned and projected onto the other, e.g., "You make me angry" or "You made me do that."

3. *Transactional:* At this level, patterns of behavior can be observed and commented upon. The reciprocal nature of the relationship is rec-

ognized, e.g., "You got angry with me, and I withdrew, and then you got angrier and I withdrew even more."

4. *Relational:* Couples who have achieved this level are aware of the underlying assumptions and rules that govern their relationship, e.g., they may know that anger is triggered by not feeling loved.

5. *Contextual:* The most important contextual factor would be awareness of how one's history, especially experiences in family of origin, affect the current relationship, e.g., a wife who is angry with her husband might be displacing old anger toward her father.

A couple can be taught these levels with the idea that the first two levels are content-oriented and linear. They may be asked to work on developing themselves in the other levels by first developing greater awareness of themselves and then discussing these ideas.

ASSUMPTIONS FACILITATING COMMUNICATION WORK

A major deficit in communication training models is in the area of the assumptions couples hold. Attempting to teach a couple new ways of communicating will be met with resistance and eventually fail unless their underlying assumptions are addressed first. By the time many couples enter therapy, a long history of miscommunication, misinterpretation, and misattribution has developed and is rigidly held in order to protect each self. Two techniques are useful in order to create a different attitudinal set and prevent the problem of miscommunication, interpretation, and attribution from reoccurring: The first technique is to help the couple differentiate between intent and effect. The second is changing assumptions.

Unfortunately, many partners develop the idea that intent and effect are exactly the same, and thus a communication that was experienced as hurtful is automatically assumed to have been intended as hurtful. It is impossible to be in a close relationship without experiencing some communication as hurtful. When this experience occurs, it is essential to check out the intent of the sender. In order to do so, the couple must first understand the difference between intent and effect. The therapist can discuss these concepts until the couple understand the difference.

Examples of how these may differ are very useful. In one case, whenever a wife asked her husband how he felt, he became angry and withdrew. He would counter her question with the response that she was trying to put him down because she was more articulate with her feelings. The fact was that he was the one ascribing hurtful intent to her because he was hurt by her question. The husband had been repeatedly punished whenever he expressed a feeling in his family of origin. The hurt he experienced over simply being asked how he felt was deeply rooted in his history and not in his wife's efforts to understand his feelings. Once they were able to check out her intent, the negative attributions made about the other stopped.

The ability to differentiate intent versus effect is essential in teaching the technique of effective listening, which is described later. Differentiating intent and effect results in cognitive restructuring. Rather than thinking, "Because that message hurt, she or he must have wanted to hurt me," the partner now thinks, "I am feeling hurt by that message; what did my partner intend to say and why am I feeling the way I am?"

The second technique is preparatory for all the others and is also designed to change assumptions. Many couples enter treatment assuming the other person does not care about them, wants to hurt them and, in spite of their best efforts, will never really be able to understand or be understood.

The therapist may suggest that both partners adopt three new assumptions to help their relationship:

1. The assumption of commitment;
2. The assumption of good will and intent; and
3. The assumption of understanding.

The first assumption highlights the fact that the couple are committed to each other and to the therapeutic process. This assumption should of course be checked out and validated before proceeding. The second assumption addresses some of the issues in differentiating intent and effect. The partners need to believe goodwill exists in the relationship. This assumption draws out their sense of caring for one another. They learn that even though a statement may be hurtful, its intent was not necessarily to hurt the other.

The third assumption is that of understanding. When couples begin therapy, they often feel their partner does not care about them or understand them. Then when a miscommunication occurs, the partner is ready to give up on the relationship and the communication stops. The point of this assumption is that no matter how muddled the communication becomes, if the partners keep trying, they will at the very least be able to understand each other. The assumption normalizes miscommunication and implies that communication is a difficult, time-consuming process. This assumption does not imply agreement. The therapist should explain how understanding the other person does not mean agreement with the other person's perception or giving in to what she or he wants. Most couples will readily agree to these assumptions. The couple should remind themselves of these assumptions every day and then every time they feel their communication is deteriorating.

CREATING A CONTEXT FOR COMMUNICATION

Effective communication requires a context with three basic structural elements. This context is taught and modeled in the therapist's office and then extended outside the office. Thus, the first technique involves teaching the couple how to create the context.

The first element is to *talk to each other*. Do not talk through other people or things. In the therapist's office the task is to keep the partners focused on each other. The therapist should be like a coach on the sidelines providing feedback and directives. At home, the couple need to speak directly to each other without using the children or others to talk for them. They should not use the TV or other activities to dilute the intensity of their interactions.

Communication should be as *free of distraction* as possible. The couple should be taught how to create "islands of experience" with each other by establishing boundaries around the dyad and setting limits when others attempt to intrude on those boundaries.

A second element of the context is *proximity* and *contact*. Partners should not attempt to talk from room to room or on the run. They need to move close together and give each other strong eye contact. In the office contact needs to be monitored and strengthened when necessary. It is useful to have the couple agree on a talking place and time. The place should be comfortable, free of distraction, and associated with pleasant activities. Touching, if only hand to hand, or fingertip to fingertip, can create even more intensity in the experience.

Third, *communication is a process and takes time*. A couple should not expect to resolve every problem in five to 15 minutes or to build a relationship in such short bursts. The couple will need to make a commitment to talk on a regular basis every day. At first, the time spent talking at home should be short and gradually lengthened as they become more successful communicators. If a regular time is not established due to fluctuating schedules, then after each talk a time could be agreed upon for their next communication. Consistency and repetition are important to the successful learning of new communication skills.

COMMUNICATION TECHNIQUES

For this section, we will describe the combination of techniques that usually promotes improved communication. Conversely, these techniques tend to diminish or to eliminate many of the common problems found in communication. These problems will be treated in the next section on obstacles to effective communication.

"I" Statements

Each partner should be encouraged to make "I" statements. "I" statements refer to: "I" think, feel, believe, wish, wonder, and so on. An "I" statement reflects the fact that the speaker is taking responsibility for self. On the other hand, "you" statements (you said, you did) are blaming or provoke defensive reactions. "It" statements (e.g., it seemed to me) are either too logical, impersonal, or vacuous to be helpful. Each partner should practice using "I" language, avoiding "you" and "it" language. Whenever they catch themselves using the latter two forms, they should stop and convert the idea to "I" language. Each partner should monitor self and be open to reminders that he or she has lapsed into other styles without getting caught in blaming the other partner when a lapse is made.

Listening

Many couples will state that their problem is one of not talking or communicating enough. There are times when it is useful to reframe this statement by saying that the problem is not one of talking, but one of knowing how to listen. Listening is more than sitting quietly, nodding, or saying um-uh now and then. Listening means letting the sender know what was heard and how the statement was interpreted. The listener's responsibility is to reflect back the context and affect that was registered. The *content* (literal) is the meaning that was extracted, while *affect* refers to the emotion stated or inferred in the statement. Examples of what a listener might say include:

> "I heard you say you felt hurt because of my comment regarding what you said to your mother."
>
> "I heard you say you felt okay about my comment, but the way you said it gave me the feeling you were sorry."
>
> "I interpreted what you said to mean that you really do want to do it, but your body language said to me that you weren't sure."

The purpose of reflective listening is for the couple to share the same meaning. Words by themselves are not always sufficient to communicate meaning, especially in cases where affect is essential as part of the understanding. The sender needs to provide a clear message that includes a statement of feeling. The sender should not assume the receiver will automatically know his or her feelings. It is the responsibility of the sender to communicate both affect as well as content. The couple need to be trained to follow a format that goes something like this: "I'm feeling ____ because of ____." In other words, make an "I" statement. Once the sender has been coached to make this kind of statement, the receiver is next coached to reflect back the affect and content.

If the reflected statement is accurate, then the discussion may proceed. However, the reflected statement may be highly discrepant with the intended communication. If this happens, the couple start the cycle over again of stating the thought and having it reflected back. When the communication has failed, many couples feel frustrated and want to give up or start blaming each other. An assumption couples make is that communication should be easy and problem-free. This assumption should be checked out with the couple and if it is present, it should be discussed.

Additionally, when couples begin to blame, the whole process comes to a halt. Blaming should not be permitted. Miscommunications need to be normalized. The couple need to see themselves as being on the same team with each partner willing to help the other when a miscommunication occurs. The therapist may predict miscommunications as a way to prepare the couple for dealing with these occurrences.

Another common problem occurs when the sender gives contradictory verbal and nonverbal messages but denies that such messages were sent because of a lack of awareness. The couple need to know that such communications are going to take place and be given a strategy to handle mixed messages. Assuming the receiver has accurately detected a discrepancy and reflected it back, the sender may continue to deny certain feelings. For example, a husband might deny that he is angry, although his nonverbal behavior reveals this feeling to the partner and the therapist. The receiver should be taught to reflect back the *specific behavior* that conveyed the feeling. In this example, the wife might say, "I thought you were feeling angry because your voice became loud, you clenched your jaw and fist, and your face turned red." The therapist may then validate these perceptions of the receiver. If the sender continues to deny the feelings, the issue should be dealt with by the therapist by trying to explore the reason for the denial.

The therapist should also note that a denied feeling will keep resurfacing, which means further interaction will help reveal the true feeling. If the sender of a contradictory message continues to deny certain feelings at home, the couple need to have an agreement. The sender should agree to accept the feedback and think about it seriously. In most cases,, the feedback is discounted and then forgotten. The receiver must be willing to stop after providing the feedback. If he or she insists the other agree, a no-win is set up. The receiver must also consider whether he or she is reading a feeling not present. The couple may return to the matter later to try to sort it out. If they are unable to do so by the next session, then it should be worked through with the therapist.

Reflective listening is essential when a couple get trapped in what has been termed the *self-summarization syndrome*. Couples need to be taught about this concept. The concept refers to each partner saying essentially the same statement over and over again, usually with increasing emotional intensity.

Self-summarization is a misguided attempt to get the other person to understand. Repeating the same message does not create understanding. Interrupting this destructive process by using reflective listening will change the interaction. One partner might suggest starting over by going back to the original point and asking for a reflective statement. Self-summarization usually occurs when a partner fails to respond in an appropriate way, but it may also occur when an individual has a fixed agenda and will not consider negotiation and compromise. In these situations the only voice the person hears is the one in his or her own head.

For example, the husband may have the agenda of proving his wife wrong. All of his statements will be designed to prove his point. His wife might try to respond, but he is so fixed in his agenda he cannot hear her statements.

The therapist can help couples learn about these obstacles and learn how to work through them in the session. They may then begin to practice at home. When communication techniques fail to correct self-summarization, it is time to explore for hidden agendas. Using this concept alerts the couple to the existence of hidden agendas and may help them to do this type of exploration if they become hopelessly stuck.

Validation

Validation is related to "I" statements and reflective listening. To be validated means to be understood as a person. The opposite of validation is discounting. Discounting means being ignored, misunderstood, or told that one felt or said something she or he did not. In other words, this type of misinterpretation occurs when certain feelings or words are wrongly ascribed to a person. This concept is known as mind raping (e.g., I know you really felt hostile even though you deny it). Couples often confuse validation with agreement, thinking that if they see the other person's point of view, they must agree with him or her. It is possible to validate another person without agreeing.

The first step in communication is to validate the other person. Then and only then can a discussion be held over differing perceptions, beliefs, opinions, and so on. When the couple try to skip the validation phase, they inevitably end up arguing over the content in an effort to get validated. They assume agreement is the same as validation once again. Confusing these concepts can be lethal to communication. The therapist must teach the couple how to validate and still be able to disagree or see things in different ways. The therapist should constantly monitor communication in the session in order to point out when validation is needed.

Editing

Written communication is usually clearer and more concise than the spoken word because the former has been thoroughly edited. Editing has several useful functions in couples' verbal communication. First, when dealing with a difficult topic, it is best for partners to think through what they want to say before they say it. The couple can be instructed in the use of *mental rehearsal* as a way to prepare for a discussion. This involves carrying out a mental dialogue designed to sharpen the ideas the person wants to communicate. Second, one can never say all that one thinks, nor should one have to. Extraneous, distracting, nonthematic comments only confuse the process of communication. The couple need to stay focused on the theme or problem. Each partner also knows what kinds of comments "push the other's button." These comments distract the couple by reengaging them in a discussion with no end. Both must agree to edit out comments designed to create conflict and sabotage the process. Each individual must also try not to take the bait if such a comment is made.

Time

Communication is a process that takes time. Couples need to learn that good communication requires not just their energy, commitment, and understanding, but also their time. They must learn how to create time to communicate. Communication should not be compressed to fit their time, but time should be expanded to fit the need to communicate. Getting couples to make dates or appointments is helpful. Sometimes the block of time will be insufficient, requiring one or more session on the same topic. The idea of doing a little at a time helps to dispel the myth that every conversation should bring about closure. When communication is extended, the need for continuity is absolute. Both partners must know when the dialogue will continue.

OBSTACLES TO EFFECTIVE COMMUNICATION

The couple must be taught how to communicate effectively and be coached in the session. Effective communication does not just happen. It is a skill that can be taught in a systematic way. The role of practice can be emphasized repeatedly as each session begins. A review might be done of skills that are in the process of being acquired. These skills will not work unless the couple also know what obstacles prevent them from communicating more effectively. They should be aware of some of the common obstacles. This information will allow each partner to do a personal self-analysis and to agree to self-monitor in order to stop destructive habits. A few of the major obstacles are reviewed below.

Mind reading.

Mind reading refers to the idea that one really knows what the partner is thinking, feeling, and so on, without checking out those assumptions. In other words, a partner's assumption is elevated to the level of reality. The therapist may ask partners to think about how they know when they are mind reading and agree to check out their assumptions. The therapist can ask partners to think about what signals, both internal and external, tell them they are mind reading. An internal signal might be a common assumption a partner makes when certain events are happening. An external signal could be as simple as giving legitimacy to the idea that the other person said, "I never said that."

Personalization.

This concept pertains to attacking the person as well as the problem. The problem should be defined in terms of what a person does, not who he or she is. Thus, when discussing a problem in the relationship, the couple should stay focused on the behavior and not attack each other personally. Attacking the other person's character or blaming the other is counterproductive. The two most common types of personalizations are labeling ("you're stupid") and generalizing ("you never listen to me").

Distracting.

There are two ways of distracting. One involves leaving the theme of the discussion by bringing up other past, present, and predicted future problems. The couple should adopt the rule of staying on one topic at a time. A related distraction involves one person bringing up an issue and the other person bringing up another issue, and so on. This strategy is one of attack and counterattack.

Polarizing Language.

Certain concepts in our language only serve to polarize couples. These include right versus wrong, always and never, truth versus lie. Language that is black and white can be eliminated. We teach couples that these concepts are polarizing, judgmental, and trouble-making. A simple rule is to ask them not to use these terms when they speak. They may think in these terms, if they must, just avoid expressing them.

The couple will then be forced to find other language. They might be encouraged to use terms such as opinions, beliefs, perceptions, feelings, values, likes, and so on. For example, a wife might say she thinks oral sex is wrong, which implies there is something wrong with him for suggesting it. He might reply that it isn't wrong and that something is wrong with her for not wanting it. They are now polarized around the issue of rightness and wrongness. Had she said she didn't like it because it made her feel embarrassed, then a discussion of her feelings could take place.

CONCLUSION

The practice of communication skills training with couples appears deceptively simple. This chapter has demonstrated the myriad factors involved in carrying out this task effectively. Once the therapist has a grasp of these techniques, it is then a matter of monitoring the communication process, assessing it moment-to-moment, and intervening actively and directively when communication fails. This last requirement of active, immediate, and directive intervention may not be a comfortable role for the therapist. A reexamination of the therapist's own beliefs and methods of working may be needed if these simple techniques are to be used effectively.

Chapter 11

Conflict Resolution

Conflict is inevitable in every close relationship. Some couples exhibit their conflict openly and directly while others attempt to deny and suppress or exhibit their conflict covertly. The question is not whether conflict exists in a couple, but how they manage conflict when it arises. Virtually every couple coming for treatment is in a state of conflict. They may be in conflict over a variety of issues, from expectations, needs, and wants, to money, sex, children, in-laws, and so on. The conflict may be expressed overtly or covertly and with varying degrees of emotional intensity. When the level of intensity is high and the couple lack the skills to successfully resolve the conflict, the first task of the therapist is to deescalate the feelings, to teach the couple conflict resolution skills, and to help them resolve their particular issues.

The exception to this approach would be when the level of intensity is so high and the need to blame each other is so entrenched that the couple are not yet ready to work together. It is best in these situations to see the partners separately until the level of anger can be reduced and the blaming can be stopped. Of course, in cases involving spouse abuse, the type of conflict must be carefully assessed; in cases where the conflict and anger is instrumental or purposeful, couples therapy should not be undertaken (Mack, 1989).

The first step in helping the couple to deal with conflict is to inform and help them to recognize that conflict exists in all close relationships. This fact helps to normalize the existence of conflict. Some couples have the idea that their marriage should be conflict-free. In their minds, any hint of conflict means they have made a serious mistake or failed. The therapist can point out that it is not a question of whether conflict exists, but rather whether the couple have managed it destructively or constructively. The couple can be asked directly, "How do the two of you manage conflict?" The therapist is probably going to hear that conflict results in getting stuck and unresolved hurt and angry feelings. At this point, the therapist can begin the change process by suggesting the idea that conflict can be a constructive force in their relationship. Toward this end the therapist may point out how constructive management of conflict can help each of them get what she or he wants, allow each of them to be heard, understood, and respected, and lead to a sense of competence and closeness.

This initial discussion of conflict is designed to change a couple's attitude that conflict is bad and can only have destructive consequences. In addition to the work done in the sessions and the homework, it is useful at the outset to use some bibliotherapy. Although a number of popular books are available on this topic, we generally ask our couples to read *The Dance of Anger* by Harriet Goldhor Lerner and *Your Perfect Right* by Alberti and Emmons. The second book is not exclusively about assertiveness in couples but covers many of the basics, including communication techniques, conflict resolution, and anger.

Before proceeding to talk more about what the therapist does, it is essential to consider how the therapist uses his or her self in dealing with conflict. Beginning therapists are often afraid of losing control of a session or of not knowing how to manage intense conflict. The therapist may have the mistaken idea that his or her job is to prevent or minimize conflict and consequently rescue the couple from their conflict. Some therapists will experience a strong countertransference reaction in which they fear anger emerging in the session because of their own difficulties-in experiencing anger. All of these possible reactions mean the therapist must believe what she or he is proposing and be free of fear of conflict and anger. The therapist may need to seek supervision or therapy to deal with personal issues. Conflict resolution is actually not that difficult a process, yet we have seen many beginning marital therapists find it impossible to implement this type of approach due to their own personal limitations. The therapist can keep a watchful eye on himself or herself to determine whether she or he is avoiding, minimizing, or denying the conflict and anger present in the couple.

ANGER

Conflict and anger are intimately related. Where there is conflict, there is usually anger. It is usually the anger that frightens the couple and the therapist. Anger is associated with losing control and being destructive.

Much of what has been emphasized in conflict-resolution work focuses on the mechanics of resolving conflict in a behavioral way. It is assumed these skills will reduce anger, but this approach does not address the problem of dealing with conflict which begins with anger. In working on this problem, a significant amount of time needs to be spent exploring attitudes, beliefs, and feelings before the behavioral work is started.

Our first task then is to help the couple understand the meaning and function of anger in their relationship. A number of questions help reveal the meaning of anger. These questions may be asked as the exploratory process unfolds. They should not be asked as a simple list of questions.

MEANING AND FUNCTION OF ANGER

1. What is anger?
2. What does it mean when you are angry?
3. What does it mean when you are angry with your partner?
4. What does it mean when your partner is angry?
5. What does it mean when your partner is angry with you?
6. How do you respond to your partner's anger?
7. How do you respond to your own anger?
8. How do you let your partner know you are angry?
9. How long does your anger usually last?
10. What other feelings are associated with anger?

The meanings attributed to anger are derived from several sources. The two most important are the experiences with one's mate and the experiences in the family of origin. Getting some history from the couple will reveal their beliefs and attitudes about anger. If a person's partner uses anger destructively, that fact will certainly influence the partner's perception of what anger means. Family of origin is also a strong factor in developing this belief system. Children learn a great deal about anger and conflict from what they see, or fail to see, in their parents behavior. The strength of this influence cannot be overstated. It is therefore useful to know what those experiences were for each partner. Some questions that are helpful include the folowing.

ANGER GENOGRAM

1. How did your parents deal with anger/conflict?
2. Did you see your parents work through anger/conflict?

3. When members of your family (name each one) got angry, how did others respond?
4. What did you learn about anger from each of your parents?
5. When a parent was angry with you, what did you feel/do?
6. When you got angry, who listened or failed to listen to you?
7. How did members of your family respond when you got angry?
8. Who was allowed and not allowed to be angry in your family?
9. What is your best/worst memory about anger in the family?
10. Was anyone ever seriously hurt when someone got angry?

These questions often reveal two patterns in the family of origin. In one pattern, a member of the family, usually the father, is the only person allowed to be overtly angry. In many of these cases, this pattern is associated with drinking. Father used anger to manipulate, control, and express his aggression. Mother and other members responded in fear, not knowing whether Father would lose control. The adult children might use this same pattern or might be so frightened of their own anger or that of others that they go to great lengths to avoid anger and its expression.

The other typical pattern is the family that attempts to deny anger and conflict. Children from these families do not understand their experience of anger nor that of their partners. Thus anger is an unknown and fearful feeling and often is out of awareness.

The type of training one experiences in the family of origin may actually play a significant role in the selection of one's mate. A partner who grew up in a home pervaded by anger might choose a mate who appears to be devoid of anger, perhaps of all feelings. Another partner might choose a mate perceived as weak and dependent so she or he can safely displace old, unresolved feelings of anger. Helping partners understand these early experiences can be validating and enlightening. They might have been told as children that they should never be angry, which invalidated their experience and led them to question and doubt their perception of the world. They may be unconsciously repeating old patterns or carrying out a mission for a parent. The therapist may see the same dynamic in the couple that was present in the parents. These unconscious scripts and repetitions cannot be effectively treated with a set of behavior-based skills. This work involves family-of-origin exploration, awareness, and an understanding of psychodynamics.

Another facet of understanding the meaning of anger is how it can be used as a shield to protect the person from experiencing feelings that are more difficult or painful. In short, the overtly expressed and felt anger may act as a defense and, at the same time, the anger may serve to give the person a sense of power, energy, and control. Anger may be used to cover up many feelings, and the therapist can explore what these other feelings might be. In many cases, the client will not know, which makes some interpretations necessary. Some of the common feelings underlying anger are frustration, guilt, sadness, depression, powerlessness, dependency, and mistrust. The therapist should keep these possibilities in mind and explore those which appear plausible.

Many partners are not in touch with these feelings or find it unacceptable to feel or to express the underlying feeling. For example, one man from a cold and rejecting family entered his marriage with strong unresolved dependency needs. Yet, he could not admit that he needed anyone or wanted anything. He could not ask for what he wanted out of fear of not getting it, and being rejected, so he expected his wife to automatically know and give him what he desperately wanted. He became chronically angry toward her for failing to meet his unexpressed needs.

There are two feelings that deserve special note. One is hurt. When there is anger there is almost always hurt. Hurt, unlike anger, usually elicits an emphatic response, yet it is difficult for many partners to say they feel hurt.

The other feeling, which has been grossly ignored in professional writing, is fear. Organisms have an innate response to fear, which leads to fleeing or fighting. This fight or flight response accounts for much of our behavior during conflict, that is, a fear response once elicited leads to withdrawing or to attacking. This explanation may be offered to the couple in order to explore sthe basis for fears that are elicited. What is so fascinating about this concept is that some of the fears are related to intimacy and were described in Chapter 8.

For example, a partner may have been reared in a destructive family where he felt neglected and abandoned. This fear follows him to his current relationship. As this person gets closer to his partner, a paradoxical situation occurs. He wants closeness, yet wanting closeness in the past was associated with rejection. During conflict, the partner's fear of rejection is unconsciously triggered and results in an angry fight. This type of trigger reaction is the reason we say skills alone will not resolve the problem. The fears of intimacy we have identified are useful to explore as part of the underlying force driving the anger.

Functions of Anger

In the previous section it was pointed out that anger may result from a fear of intimacy. Anger then may function to regulate distance in a relationship. When a partner is getting too close and eliciting unconscious fear, there is a need to create distance. Because the need is unknown and fear is experienced as anger, the partner has no conscious methods to negotiate for the distance. A fight can serve to alleviate the underlying feeling of fear by creating distance. Conversely, when partners become too distant, anger can be used in order to serve as a means of gaining the attention of and interaction with the other partner.

Anger may also be used in a similar manner to test the degree of commitment in a relationship. If a partner believes her partner may reject or abandon, then it is possible to test this belief by trying to push the person away through anger. If he keeps coming back, then the partner knows she will not be rejected. In more extreme cases, the partner may discover that he or she can engage in highly disruptive behavior because of the other person's high dependency needs. Such situations occur among people with low self-esteem, especially those in relationships with addictions. The alcoholic husband may be chronically abusive to his codependent wife. She is in need of therapy just as much as he is because of her dependence on the relationship.

Anger may be used to assert power and control in a relationship, and the partner who needs to bolster his or her sense of power by controlling another will usually find that anger is an effective method. This partner will also choose someone who can be intimidated by anger. The therapist should consider the individual dynamics and pathology of such a partner. These partners may fall into diagnostic categories such as narcissistic, paranoid, aggressive, and sociopathic.

Anger may also function in at least two healthy ways in a relationship. When a boundary is violated, anger is likely to emerge. The boundary may be related to any subsystem of the couple's relationship. The two most common boundaries are associated with self and marriage. In the first case, an individual may feel she or he is having rights violated. For example, a couple might argue that the husband can have an evening to work at home before a major presentation the next day. As the evening unfolds, his wife begins to interrupt him over things that could have waited. He might assert himself with anger to let her know that she violated the agreement they made.

In the second case, anger may stem from a violation of marital boundary. In one case, a young married couple presented in therapy because the husband would tell his parents things that his wife considered private. They had never discussed this problem calmly in order to clarify expectations, but they had fought over it many times after getting certain information back from his parents. It is useful to help the couple think about both the meaning and function of their anger. Once they have developed some awareness, it is much easier and usually much more successful to learn and to utilize fair fighting skills.

The therapist and the couple must also recognize anger when it is disguised as something else. Anger is not always expressed openly as anger. Anger may be thinly disguised or so well disguised that even the therapist has trouble seeing it. The thinnest disguise for anger from most therapists' perspective is passive-aggressive behavior. As the term implies, the aggression is expressed indirectly or passively. Some of the common methods of being passive-aggressive are forgetting, procrastinating, misunderstanding, and overreading the other person's behavior.

An example of passive-agressive behavior involved a husband who forgot to pick his wife up at a designated time. He claimed he forgot the time. Procrastinating doing something for one's partner is another expression of anger, for example, a wife had promised to organize some household files and six months later they still weren't done. Misunderstanding and overreading the partner's behavior are similar. If the other partner has been clear, but the first continues to misunderstand, then a payoff is to be found in not understanding. Likewise, a partner may read certain things into the partner's behavior and, despite the partner's protest that it is not true, insist that it is in order to justify the behavior.

A second way to disguise anger is to take a position of righteousness. By asserting that one is right, moral, true, good, and so on, the other person is cast in the role of being wrong, immoral, deceitful or lying, and bad. This hostile and indirect way of putting one's partner down allows the partner to try to get away with his or her anger.

A third method to hide anger is through self-victimization. The victimized partner (e.g., "You absolutely must take care of me and not upset me") may either pretend to be sick or develop psychosomatic problems. In one of our cases, a woman had married a distant, cold, and self-righteous husband who was totally inaccessible. His wife developed numerous aches and pains that could never be medically diagnosed. Because of her history, she had not learned to express anger in direct form, and her various ailments served to get her husband's attention and also as a way for her to express her discontents, albeit indirectly.

The final method is the most difficult to see as anger because in this strategy, the partner uses the ploy of reason and rationality to vent anger. These partners tend to be obsessive-compulsive personalities who use intellectualization as both a defense and as an offense.

One of our cases demonstrates this point in a dramatic way. The wife had been decorating the house and decided to purchase new curtains. When the husband discovered how much money she had spent, he was unquestionably upset. However, when he discussed the curtains with his wife, he gave her one logical reason after another why the curtains had to be returned. He even claimed they lacked the proper thermal properties. In addition, he said she could not be trusted to make good decisions without him, so he decided to take away all of her credit cards. When initially confronted in therapy about the denial of his anger, he vehemently denied any feeling of anger toward her. This case points out how difficult it can be to help partners recognize and acknowledge their anger.

Giving clients permission and providing a safe, secure environment in which to explore facilitates the expression of feelings. Although the focus may be on one partner, the reactions of the other partner should be monitored. Partners may actually collude to keep the pattern intact. They may be too frightened of anger to deal with it openly.

GENERAL PRINCIPLES OF FAIR FIGHTING

In order to have a fair fight, a number of rules must be remembered. A fair fight starts with the individual who has the problem doing a self-assessment. Prior to saying anything to the partner, it is important to sort out one's own feelings. Earlier in this chapter it was suggested that anger may only be the tip of an iceberg which contains a variety of other feelings. During the first part of a fair fight, the feelings need to be expressed. If anger is the only expressed feeling and many others are withheld, then the other person cannot respond appropriately. In many cases, the angry person wants the partner to see how hurt she or he is, but when the partner fails to acknowledge the hurt, she or he does not get what is needed, feels frustrated, and becomes even angrier. Taking time to explore one's feeling in some depth helps to facilitate the expression of those feelings.

The second major task of the angry person is to identify the source of the anger before beginning an argument. In some cases the source of anger is clearly unrealistic. For example, a man might be angry because his wife spent a few minutes talking to another man at a party. He expected her to stay with him and talk only to couples or other women. This expectation is unrealistic and engenders anger. It is each partner's responsibility to determine whether his or her anger has a rational basis. If it does not, then the partner needs to use the cognitive therapy approach (see Chapter 12) discussed in this volume. The partner may be informed about the feeling and the fact that the other partner is attempting to take responsibility for it by changing his or her thinking.

On a practical level several ideas need to be discussed before the actual steps to fair fighting are reviewed. First, the couple need to be reminded that in a fair fight the attitude must be one of win-win. This attitude consists of being willing to give up something in order to bring about a compromise. The therapist can point out that unless each person feels she or he has given up something, they probably do not have a compromise solution.

Second, fair fighting is a skill. It takes time to acquire a skill. During the process, mistakes will be made. When mistakes are made, the partners should not blame each other or give up. In fact, they may agree to help each other by pointing out times when the partner deviates from the rules. The couple should begin to use these rules with issues that are not emotionally laden. We suggest the couple divide these issues into three categories—cool, warm, and hot. They begin to use fair fighting with the cool issues in the session, practice more at home, and then move on to the warm issues. The couple can be reminded that fair fighting requires practice, practice, and more practice.

The third rule deals with time. Fair fighting requires time. Ideally, the couple would be able to discuss a disagreement as soon as it occurs. This idea assumes they have plenty of time. The reality is that many fights occur when there is not time to talk or the conditions are not right (e.g., when guests are over). In these situations, the partner may express the feeling discretely and agree to talk later. A fixed time needs to be set in order to contain the problem. If a time is not set, the partner is likely to keep bringing up the anger. When the discussion does take place, resolving the fight may take more time than was allotted. A fight can be broken up into segments. Some disagreements take many hours to resolve. Fights should not be hurried in order meet some time limit or the need for quick resolution.

Having a fair fight assumes the anger is under conscious control. Sometimes a fight will deteriorate into a destructive situation because of escalating anger and decreasing self-control. A rule we suggest is that either partner may call a time out during an argument unilaterally and without question. The partner who is getting angry may call a time-out to cool off. The partner on the receiving end of the anger may call a time-out because he or she is afraid of the anger or sees a deterioration in the argument. The cooling-off period should be as short as possible but as long as is needed to bring the emotion down to a manageable level. The person who calls the time-out is also responsible for setting the time to resume the argument.

The couple should understand and be in agreement with these ideas before proceeding to the mechanics of fair fighting. Fair fighting consists

---

ESSENTIAL DO'S AND DON'TS

1. Be specific when you introduce a gripe.
2. Don't just complain, no matter how specifically; ask for a reasonable change that will relieve one gripe at a time.
3. Confine yourself to one issue at a time. Otherwise, without professional guidance, you may skip back and forth, evading the hard ones.
4. Always consider compromise. Remember, your partner's view of reality is just as real as yours, even though you may differ. There are not any totally objective realities.
5. Do not allow counterdemands to enter the picture until the original demands are clearly understood, and there has been a clear-cut response to them.
6. Never assume that you know what your partner is thinking until you have checked out the assumption in plain language; never assume or predict how your partner will react, or what your partner will accept or reject.
7. Never put labels on your partner. Do not make sweeping, labeling judgments about your partner's feelings, especially about whether or not they are real or important.
8. Sarcasm is dirty fighting.
9. Forget the past and stay with the here-and-now. What either of you did last year or month or that morning is not as important as what you are doing and feeling now. The changes you ask cannot possibly be retroactive. Hurts, grievances, and irritations should be brought up at the very earliest moment, otherwise your partner may suspect that they may have been saved carefully as weapons.

of a number of do's and don'ts. The first task of the therapist is to make each partner responsible for how he or she fights. We give each partner a copy of the *Essential Do's and Don'ts* (see box). They are asked to read this list and rank order the items where they have trouble. In the next session, each partner is asked to talk about bad habits and how she or he might change the habits. The therapist may praise their constructive comments as well as offer additional suggestions to help overcome habits that are not helpful.

The next task is to go over the steps in constructive conflict resolution (see box on Steps to Fair Fighting). These steps are broken down so they are easy to understand. The therapist may wish to point out that steps 1 through 4 deal with feelings about the problems and mutual understanding. Before a problem is "solved," it is essential to acknowledge the other person's feelings about it first. Couples make two common mistakes in this area. The first, as we have implied, is to fail to discuss the feelings about the problem rather than the problem itself. Acknowledging the feelings of the other does not imply accepting the other's position. This fact often keeps partners from acknowledging the other because they equate acknowledgment of the other person's position with acceptance.

The fact is that in many cases the person who expressed the problem just wants to talk about his or her feelings and not about the problem. This situation frequently occurs when the problem is outside the relationship. In a typical scenario, a wife may be having a problem at work. When she tells her husband how she is feeling he begins to give advice or problem-solve. The wife in turn feels discounted emotionally. She believes he is problem solving in order to make her problem go away. The couple need to be aware of when and when not to proceed to the problem-solving steps (5–11) in this model.

As we said earlier these steps should be put into practice in the session in which the couple are working on easy issues or is just role-playing some dispute. The first session may require a half an hour to a full hour just for one argument. Once they have practiced the steps once, the pace usually increases and the steps will become less mechanical and more natural. In order to help the reader pull together the techniques described in this chapter in a systematic way, we have developed a flow chart that shows when various techniques should be used (Figure 2, p.150).

STEPS TO FAIR FIGHTING

1. The person who has the problem is responsible for bringing it up as soon as possible. Before you bring the problem up, think it through in your own mind.

2. State the problem to your partner as clearly and concretely as possible. Use the following format:
   "I am feeling *(e.g., angry)* because of *(e.g., the way you put me down at your parents' house)*."

3. It is important that you both understand the problem being brought up. The partner who is on the receiving end should reflect back what was said using the following format:
   "I hear you saying you feel _____ because of _____ ."
   After reflecting back what was said, ask clarifying questions so you know exactly what your partner meant. For example, "Describe." "Tell me." "What is it that upsets you?"

4. When both partners agree on what is being said, the first partner may proceed.

5. The partner who brings up the problem should take responsibility for offering a possible solution in terms of changes both can make (e.g., "I can make sure you know what I want. I would like to suggest you _____ .").

6. This solution can be discussed and then your partner may offer a counterproposal. Again, the solution should involve changes *both* of you can make.

7. Discuss several options until you agree that one proposal is most *workable* (not right or wrong, but workable).

8. Once you have agreed on an idea, proceed to talk about how you will put it into action. This means being able to clearly answer the questions: Who will do what, when, and how.

9. Once everything has been worked out, think about what could happen to undermine it. Each of you can think of how you might sabotage the agreement.

10. Working through a conflict stirs up a lot of feelings because it means you had to give up something. Congratulate each other for the hard work and willingness to compromise. Reaffirm your relationship in as many ways as possible. You have good reason to celebrate.

11. Agree to come back to this problem after some specific period of time to reassess how the agreement is working. You may need to change it or fine-tune part of it.

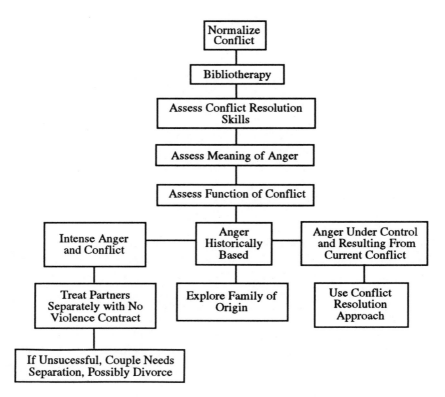

Figure 2. Flow Chart for Conflict Resolution

DEEPLY ROOTED CONFLICT

The fair fighting approach presented here is highly effective for most arguments. When the conflict resolution described above fails to work, it is usually because a hidden agenda exists in the couple's relationship. What does the hidden agenda actually mean? In conflict-resolution models, a basic assumption is that the couple lack the interpersonal or social skills needed to fight constructively. Of course, this assumption does not take into account the intergenerational factors described in this chapter.

Conflict needs to be understood within the Intersystem Approach as having multiple dimensions. Traditional conflict-resolution programs focus on the conflict from the interactional perspective. In some cases, work at the interactional and intergenerational levels is not sufficient. Couples who do not respond to a behavioral approach need to be examined from this perspective. They may carry intrapsychic issues that make them appear "impossible" or difficult to manage as a couple. In these cases, the conflict needs to be conceptualized at the individual level in terms of intrapsychic components. The conflict could be an expression of a personality disorder such as the passive-aggressive personality or as an expression of depression.

Feldman (1982) developed one of the most clinically useful intrapsychic models to account for marital conflict. In this model the underlying cause is what he calls narcissistic vulnerability. The phenomenon refers to low self-esteem, self-fragmentation, and a lack of sense of identity. This weakness in the partners leads to hypersensitivity and narcissistic expectations. The partners are very sensitive to rejection, disapproval, and criticism and have difficulty controlling their emotions and behavior. To compensate for their vulnerability, they develop unconscious expectations that the other partner will be totally admiring, attentive, loving, and so on. Because these expectations are so pervasive and unconscious, each partner is wrapped up in self and appears unempathetic to the other.

Obviously, no partner could fulfill these expectations, and so this leads to narcissistic rage and anxiety. If the process stops at this stage, the other partner becomes the scapegoat for the vulnerability. However, for some individuals the process involves a phenomenon known as projective identification. This defense mechanism involves splitting off some disowned or unacceptable part of self and projecting it onto the partner. The other person may become all good, or most commonly, all bad. The "all bad" partner holds those parts that cannot be allowed in self. Once this unacceptable material has been projected onto the other person, the projection process continues. The projector then attempts to destroy this behavior in the partner. The image of the partner is now grossly distorted and results in an unconscious escalation of conflict.

Figure 3 shows the various stages schematically, as well as the various approaches to treating different parts of the cycle. A model such as this requires in-depth, insight-oriented work over an extended period of time. When factors such as narcissistic vulnerability come into play, social skills training may be only one part of what is needed.

In addition to this model, it is useful to remember couples operate in collusion. They may both need the conflict and anger in order to protect themselves from dealing with other feelings. They may both fear intimacy and need a relationship in which intimacy is set up to be an impossibility. In examining the conflict from an intrapsychic perspective, the therapist

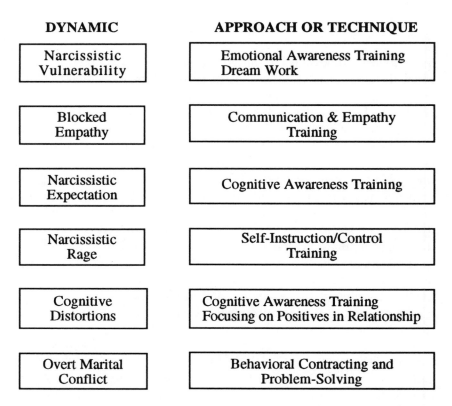

DYNAMIC	APPROACH OR TECHNIQUE
Narcissistic Vulnerability	Emotional Awareness Training Dream Work
Blocked Empathy	Communication & Empathy Training
Narcissistic Expectation	Cognitive Awareness Training
Narcissistic Rage	Self-Instruction/Control Training
Cognitive Distortions	Cognitive Awareness Training Focusing on Positives in Relationship
Overt Marital Conflict	Behavioral Contracting and Problem-Solving

Figure 3. Dynamic Processes and Treatment Techniques in Feldman's (1982) Approach. Reprinted with permission.

must explore the unconscious needs being met by maintaining the pattern of conflictual interaction.

CONCLUSION

The reduction of conflict and anger is one important barrier to couples' intimacy. Couples who move through conflict resolution successfully begin to feel a greater sense of competence and relationship bonding. They begin to realize conflict is a challenge that they can overcome as a couple. This process affirms their relationship.

The model presented in this chapter is more comprehensive than most other models (L'Abate & McHenry, 1983.) From the model presented in the flow chart, the clinician can see that we view the problem from multiple perspectives consistent with the Intersystem Approach. For example, at the individual level, we might think about the meaning of anger for the individual partner; at the interactional level, we might consider the function of the conflict for the couple; and at the intergenerational level, we might see how familial patterns of dealing with anger are being repeated. Keeping all these levels in mind gives conflict a complexity not often appreciated in working with this issue.

Chapter 12

Cognitive Techniques

The marital therapist has the choice of using interventions that are affectively, behaviorally, or cognitively oriented. The first two categories of interventions have been widely discussed in the marital therapy literature (L'Abate & McHenry, 1983). The use of cognitive interventions has received little interest in spite of the fact that cognitive approaches have been highly influential in individual psychotherapy. For the most part, cognitive approaches have only been applied to individuals. Most of Albert Ellis's (1962) early work in Rational-Emotive Therapy (RET) and Aaron Beck's (1976) work in Cognitive Therapy (CT) were individually oriented. Beck (1988) only recently discussed how cognitive therapy might be applied to couples.

The exception is Ellis and Harper's (1961b) book on how Rational-Emotive Therapy might be applied in understanding and treating marriages. These ideas clearly did not take hold in the field of marital therapy. We believe the reason for this is because they promoted RET as a singular approach, just as Beck has done with Cognitive Therapy more recently. Cognitive approaches have their utility, but they also have limitations. In fact, for most couples the use of any single approach is too narrow and ineffective. Promoting change and growth in a couple requires the clinician to use a variety of approaches and to fit the approaches to the couple, not the couple to the approach.

Although this chapter will describe cognitive techniques, we do not advocate that they be used exclusively. These techniques need to be blended with the techniques found in other chapters of this book. As Epstein (1982) pointed out, the marital therapist must be skillful in integrating the couple's internal cognitions with their overt interactions. Overt interactions would include the behavioral interchanges as well as the affective expressions of each partner.

THE THEORY

In order to use cognitive techniques, the clinician must be familiar with the basic theory and principles of both Rational-Emotive and Cognitive Therapy. Both of these theories obviously focus on cognition, that is, what and how people think. These theories postulate that behavior and affect follow from thinking. In other words, if the clinician wants to alter what a person does or how a person feels, the first step is to change the person's thinking. What has not been pointed out in the literature is the basic difference between Rational-Emotive and Cognitive theory.

The cognitive therapist focuses more on *how* the person is thinking, while the Rational-Emotive therapist focuses more on *what* the person is thinking. Thus, Rational-Emotive therapists are content-oriented and cognitive therapists are process-oriented. The combination of these two approaches is essential in as much as thinking is both content and process.

For example, a wife concluded that her husband did not love her because he was acting sad and withdrawn following the funeral of a friend. A cognitive therapist would examine the process of her thinking and might conclude she had made what is called an arbitrary inference—to draw a conclusion without substantiating evidence. A Rational-Emotive therapist would examine the statement itself and help her change the self-statement—"I absolutely must have everyone's love and approval."

RATIONAL-EMOTIVE THERAPY

Albert Ellis's (1962) basic theory consists of the A-B-C-D model. A stands for actions. An action is an event that can be observed. B refers to the person's belief or belief system. B is commonly referred to as the person's self-statement. The self-statement is what the person says (thinks) to self about A. The self-statement gives A its meaning. At the same time, it also determines C in the formula. C is the consequence of B. By consequence is meant: (1) what the person does; and (2) how the person feels. D is short for dispute. Once the person understands B is an irrational or nonproductive thought, she or he may dispute the original belief and substitute a rational or productive statement. In sum, the basic theory can be outlined as follows:

A ——————> B ——————> C ——————> D
ACTION   BELIEF   CONSEQUENCE   DISPUTE

Something happened   Self-statement   1. What you did   Seeing the original
                     What you said   2. What you felt   belief as irra-
                     to your self   tional, disputing
                     about A.   it, and substitut-
                                                         ing a rational
                                                         statement

This theory and model can be easily explained to the clients. Ideally, it is also useful to give an example—an example drawn from the clients' own experience as well as a general example. One such example involves a husband who comes home angry and begins to displace his anger onto his wife. He might be critical of her and get annoyed and angry about minor occurrences such as the house not being clean enough, supper not being ready, or his mail not being in the right place. His wife might respond to his behavior by going to another room and crying. Given her behavior, what must she be thinking about his actions? She might be making self-statements like, "It's all my fault" or "I'm a bad wife." Neither of these statements is productive. She needs to change her belief about what happened so she does not feel bad, withdraw from him, and make further assumptions about his actions. She might think, "He had a tough day and is irritable, so it's not me he is angry with but his situation."

In addition to the basic theory of RET, it is also useful to know some of the common irrational thoughts that creep into people's thinking. Ellis and Harper (1961a) have catalogued some of these thoughts in their book, *A Guide to Rational Living*. The following is a general list of these irrational thoughts, followed by some of the ways in which these thoughts get played out in couple relationships.

IRRATIONAL IDEA #1

The idea involves thinking that it is a dire necessity for an adult to be loved or approved by virtually every significant other person for everything she or he does. This thought is common in couple relationships. The partners usually expect acceptance, approval, agreement, and love for virtually everything they do. When this idea is taken to the extreme, every action is equated to love and approval. An action that does not meet the expectation is then seen as rejection and disapproval, which creates an emotionally intense situation. In couples, this irrationality can be succinctly stated as, "My partner must absolutely love and approve of everything I do." Of course, this belief is a prescription for not feeling adequately loved, since it cannot be totally and completely met.

IRRATIONAL IDEA #2

The idea involves thinking that one should be thoroughly competent, adequate, intelligent, and achieving in all possible respects. Failure, says Ellis, is construed as the worst possible crime in our society and the fear of making a mistake brings unhappiness plus a refusal to take risks. The rational individual strives to *do*, not to *do perfectly* and accepts himself or herself as a fallible creature who is imperfect because of human limitations.

In couples this idea translates into the perfect partner syndrome. The perfect partner should be able to do everything that is expected. These partners overachieve, push themselves to the limit, rarely ask for help, and pretend to be forever cheerful. One of the most destructive ways in which this particular idea manifests itself is when the partner is not only trying to do all that is expected, but also guesses (mind reads) what is expected and not expressed. In short, the partner tries to anticipate the needs of the other and creates need where none existed. In spite of striving for perfection, this partner always feels that he or she is failing.

IRRATIONAL IDEA #3

The idea involves thinking that certain acts are wrong or wicked or villainous and that people who perform such acts should be severely punished. In couples, this idea gives the partners a right to punish each other because it legitimizes the idea that when there is a victim, there is a villain. Thus, if one partner does something the other defines as wrong, the wronged partner has the right, if not the obligation, to punish the other. This situation does not allow for forgiveness—only punishment and revenge. Affairs are a classic example. The person who committed the affair is often seen as wicked, while the other partner is just an innocent bystander. By polarizing the thinking into right versus wrong, there is no way for nonaffair partners to see their roles in the marital pathology that leads to the affair. Affair partners may also believe that they deserve to be severely punished and to feel guilty.

IRRATIONAL IDEA #4

The idea involves thinking it is terrible, horrible, and catastrophic when things are not going the way one would like them to go. According to Ellis, frustration is normal and events in life can be unpleasant or unfortunate but rarely are they catastrophic unless we think they are. The rational person accepts the fact that it is too bad when things are not the way one would like them to be and one should certainly try to change or control conditions so that they become more satisfactory. However, one does realize that if changing or controlling an uncomfortable situation is impossible, one had better become resigned to its existence and stop telling oneself how awful it is.

All partners have expectations of each other. Under normal conditions the expectation is that not all expectations will be fulfilled. However, some partners enter relationships with little tolerance for frustration, disappointment, or impulse control. They are so narcissistically vulnerable that if something does not turn out their way, they feel personally injured or attacked. This type of partner makes situations into catastrophes.

In one case a husband expected his wife to keep her personal items on the chest in the bedroom in exactly the way he had shown her. When she failed to follow his instructions, his immediate reaction was to believe the marriage was a mistake and that she did not love him.

IRRATIONAL IDEA #5

The idea involves thinking human unhappiness is externally caused and is forced on one by outside people and events. The rational person realizes that virtually all human unhappiness is caused or sustained by our interpretation of things rather than by the things themselves.

Partners frequently use this idea to blame their unhappiness on the other person. By externalizing responsibility for happiness onto another, they do not have to examine their own behavior. In couple sessions, the partners may only want to talk about the other person or the relationship and never self. The other person becomes an object who acts upon them in a purported cause-effect manner. The unhappy partner is unable to see how his or her interpretation of the event or person creates the feeling.

IRRATIONAL IDEA #6

The idea involves thinking that if something is or may be dangerous or fearsome, one should be terribly occupied with and upset about it. In couples, the idea that one should be upset and preoccupied with fear is enacted in two ways that initially may appear to be opposite. The first way involves the fear of intimacy or getting too close. For many partners this fear is initially unconscious. In others it may be keenly known to them. For example, a partner who had been rejected by two previous husbands may fear rejection again. This partner may set up a situation in which she rejects first or keeps so distant that rejection is perceived as making little difference to her.

At the other end of the spectrum is the partner who fears too much distance or divorce. Partners with this concern are in a chronic state of fear over loss and being alone. Codependent partners fit this description. They marry an addicted person and stay with them because of their own fears of being alone and unlovable and because of their extremely low self-esteem.

IRRATIONAL IDEA #7

The idea involves thinking that it is easier to avoid facing many of life's difficulties and self-responsibilities than to deal with them directly. Ellis links this to our biological tendency to seek pleasure now, rather than to delay the pleasure in order to work for long-range goals, which may be more difficult to achieve. The rational individual realizes that the challenging, responsible, problem-solving life is the enjoyable life and that self-discipline is required to face difficult problems.

One of the common myths of marriage is that all will be bliss after the honeymoon; partners who ascribe to this myth assume marriage is or should be easy. Love, they believe, will be the great panacea. When confronted with the reality that relationships are difficult, require constant attention, effort, and hard work, they sometimes choose to flee through divorce, distraction in work, or substance abuse. The understanding that one builds a relationship over time is missing. Couples operating with these myths believe problems must be solved immediately; if they aren't, it means they will never be resolved. In many cases young couples believe conflict is all bad and that all problems must be solved immediately and without angry feelings. To fail in this task represents a failed marriage.

IRRATIONAL IDEA #8

The idea involves thinking that the past is all-important and that because something once strongly affected one's life, it should do so indefinitely. This idea can lead a person to overgeneralize from past events to present situations so that she or he does not look for new options, but rather transfers feelings about others from the past onto people in the present surroundings. The rational person learns from past experiences, but is not overly attached to or prejudiced by them.

Couples can use this irrational idea in a variety of ways. One way would be for a partner to focus on one specific event in the history of the relationship and use that event as the basis for the relationship. For example, a wife believed her husband had to control her sexually on their honeymoon. From that point onward she construed every comment in terms of how controlling her husband was. This line of thinking tends to be based on relationship trauma, such as a major fight, affair, or difference in values, which is never resolved and is played out again and again around different content.

Another way in which couples use this idea is to justify their behavior on the basis of childhood experiences. For example, a woman who was abused by her brother claimed she could never trust any man in spite of the fact only one man had mistreated her.

IRRATIONAL IDEA #9

The idea involves thinking that human happiness can be achieved by inertia and inaction or by passively and uncommittedly "enjoying oneself." Ellis often sees inertia as a defense against an irrational fear such as failure. Rational individuals realize that they are happiest when they are actively and vitally absorbed in creative pursuits, or when they are devoting themselves to people or projects outside of themselves.

In couples, this idea is similar to Irrational Idea #7. In this case, the partners assume no responsibility for their own happiness, expecting the other to have taken on this responsibility now. The key to treatment in such a case is to get each partner to identify and work toward taking care of their own needs. In one case a husband assumed his marriage would somehow magically cure a long-standing depression. He had not sought treatment nor taken any responsibility for his mood. He thought the occassional good feelings he felt in being with his wife would "take over his personality."

IRRATIONAL IDEA #10

The idea involves thinking that one should be quite upset over other people's problems and disturbances. Ellis says that being involved with others' problems which do not directly affect us is a way to avoid facing our own behavior and problems. Partners cross over the line of normal concern when they become engrossed in the other partner's problems in order to avoid dealing with their own.

This pattern is classic in dysfunctional couples. One partner will be defined as the sick one while the other one is the well one. What is not obvious is the pathology in the "well" partner. Frequently, these partners have selected a sick mate who actually carries their underlying problem. For example, a partner who cannot confront depression himself may marry a depressed individual.

IRRATIONAL IDEA #11

The idea involves thinking that there is a right or perfect solution to every problem and it must be found or the results will be catastrophic. There is no perfect solution and a desire for perfectionism only results in not seeing the alternative solutions. The rational person attempts to find various solutions to a problem and accepts the best answer, recognizing there is no perfect answer.

Some can get hooked on the idea of absolute right and wrong. If there is a right and wrong, then every problem has *a* right and *a* wrong answer. Such a couple is not capable of generating alternative solutions or of being creative. They think the right answer must be somewhere. It may be in logic, authority, divine wisdom, an expert, or part of family tradition. The only way to avoid this problem is to discard right and wrong thinking, replacing it with likes, preferences, needs, opinions, and so on.

IRRATIONAL IDEA #12

The idea involves thinking that one has virtually no control over one's emotions and that one cannot help feeling certain things. The rational person sees that he has enormous control over his emotions if he chooses to work at controlling them and chooses to practice saying the right kinds of sentences to himself.

Partners can claim they do not have control over how they feel. When partners make this claim, it is often with the idea that their partner should overlook their feelings because they couldn't help it or take responsibility for creating the feelings. When partners make assertions like these, they must be challenged with information on how to take control and confronted on the process of not accepting personal responsibility. Some partners believe marriage gives them permission to give up emotional control.

This list of irrational thoughts can be supplemented with a more recent list, which focuses exclusively on love and approval (Ellis, 1987).

*Irrational Beliefs About Love and Approval**

OBVIOUS OR BLATANT IRRATIONALITIES:

1. "Because I strongly desire to be approved by people I find significant, I absolutely must have their approval (and am an unlovable and worthless person if I do not)!"
2. "Because I strongly desire to be approved by people I find significant, I absolutely must ALWAYS have their approval!"
3. "Because I strongly desire to be approved by people I find significant, I absolutely must have OUTSTANDING approval!"
4. "Because I strongly desire to be approved by people I find significant, I absolutely must have TOTAL AND PERFECT approval!"

SUBTLE OR TRICKY IRRATIONALITIES:

1. "Because I strongly desire to be approved by people I find significant and BECAUSE I VERY STRONGLY WANT TO BE, I absolutely must have their approval!"
2. "Because I strongly desire to be approved by people I find significant, and BECAUSE I ONLY WANT A LITTLE APPROVAL FROM THEM, I absolutely must have it!"
3. "Because I strongly desire to be approved by people I find significant, and BECAUSE I HAVEN'T HAD MUCH LOVE AND APPROVAL FOR A LONG PERIOD OF TIME, I absolutely must have their approval!"
4. "Because I strongly desire to be loved and approved by people I find significant, and BECAUSE I HAVE BEEN WARMLY APPROVED IN THE PAST, I absolutely must have their approval now!"
5. "Because I strongly desire to be approved by people I find significant, and BECAUSE I AM A SPECIAL KIND OF PERSON, I absolutely must have their approval."
6. "Because I strongly desire to be approved by people I find significant and, BECAUSE I HAVE BEEN SO DEPRIVED IN OTHER AREAS OF MY LIFE (AS I MUST NOT BE!), I absolutely must have their approval!"

*Copyright © 1987 by the American Psychological Association. Adapted by permission.

7. "Because I strongly desire to be approved by people I find significant, and BECAUSE I FEEL SO ANXIOUS AND DEPRESSED WHEN I AM NOT APPROVED, MY POWERFUL FEELINGS OF NEEDINESS PROVE THAT I absolutely must have their approval!"
8. "Because I strongly desire to be approved by people I find significant and BECAUSE THE LACK OF THEIR APPROVAL MAKES ME BEHAVE SO BADLY, MY DYSFUNCTIONAL BEHAVIOR PROVES THAT I absolutely must have their approval!"

Notice how in this list statements are framed in terms of absolute *musts*. Ellis has pointed out how statements that include *must, ought,* and *should* create trouble. Whenever these words are detected, they need to be immediately challenged. The client can be asked to eliminate these words and insert statements such as "I would prefer" or "I would like." A simple change in wording can create a major change in thinking and lessen the severity of consequences. For example, changing "I must have his approval" to "I would like his approval" brings about a lessening of the behavioral and emotional consequences if approval is not forthcoming.

Ellis and Harper (1961) laid the foundation for the application of RET to couples. They proposed that marital problems occur when spouses have unrealistic (irrational) expectations of each other and then make extreme negative self-statements on the basis of these expectations. To illustrate, a husband might think his wife should spend *all* her time with him. When she fails to do so, he thinks because she does not want to spend her time with him, she cannot love him. The clinician's work is to expose the irrational thinking and the negative judgment made on the basis of it and replace the irrational thoughts with more productive thinking.

COGNITIVE THERAPY

This approach to treatment was developed by Aaron Beck (1976) and popularized by David Burns (1980) in his book entitled *Feeling Good.* Beck and Burns focus on the process of thinking. They both assert certain ways of thinking may be automatic. In other words, the person automatically uses a habitual pattern of thinking in assessing a situation. These patterns in turn create what are called *cognitive distortions.*

The most important part of cognitive theory is an understanding of the types of cognitive distortions. Burns (1980) has described these in terms which are easily comprehensible for the lay person. The chapter in his book (Chapter 4) that reviews these concepts is essential bibliotherapy for the couple when this approach is being used. The following list summarizes the cognitive distortions that Burns considers most common:

1. *All or nothing. Either/or thinking.* The person's thinking is dichotomous and polarized. A wife might ask her husband to sit down and talk with her. When he agrees to talk—but at a later time—she might conclude, "He never wants to talk with me."

2. *Overgeneralization.* A single event may be viewed as establishing a pattern over one's marriage. A husband brought his wife flowers only to be told there was not a vase in which to put them. The husband generalized from this event that he could never bring his wife anything because she would find some problem with it.

3. *Mental filter.* This distortion involves allowing one negative event to color all subsequent events. This distortion means all new experiences are filtered through the original negative experience. For example, after many years of a husband never being turned down sexually, his wife finally became sexually assertive and said no on one occasion. Thereafter, the husband believed his wife was never really interested in him sexually.

4. *Discounting positives.* A positive change is not accepted as real and the negatives continue to receive attention. A husband started to give his wife compliments after starting therapy. His wife discounted his remarks as an act designed to get her off his back and to placate the therapist.

5. *Jumping to conclusions.* This distortion involves drawing inferences without checking out the other person's intent. A separated couple were working on getting back together. Because the primary cause of the separation had been defined as sexual, the wife believed the first time they had sex would be a pass-fail test for her. She had assumed he would be grading her performance and determining the outcome of the marriage based on one sexual encounter.

6. *Magnification.* An event is given more emotional weight than it should. A wife had lunch with a male colleague whom she knew her husband envied. He reacted to the lunch with great jealousy, claiming the other man had it all and he had nothing, including his wife's attention.

7. *Emotional reasoning.* This idea deals with emotionally based logic. The person believes that because he or she feels a certain way, life must really be that way. A divorced man said, "My wife rejected me, my mother rejected me, I feel rejected by women. Women do not really like men, they just use them and reject them." The emotional reality becomes reality. If something feels a certain way, it must *be* that way.

8. *"Shoulding."* This distortion involves raising a *wish, want* or *preference* to the level of a *should.* In one case, a husband wanted his second wife to have the same close relationship to his children that his first wife had. He insisted that she *should* make this happen.

9. *Labeling.* This distortion involves putting a label on another person rather than being descriptive and behavioral. A husband made an insensitive remark to his wife. Rather than saying, "Your remark hurt me and was insensitive," she said, "You are an insensitive person." The label placed on the person usually describes the unacceptable behavior; the label serves to magnify the perceived negative intent.

10. *Personalizing.* Taking responsibility or blame for an event that is outside of one's control. A couple went on their dream vacation. The husband acted depressed and angry throughout. His wife said, "I should have known what to do to cheer him up. I'm sure I did something to make this happen." She accepted responsibility for his moods although she had no control over them.

Cognitive Therapy and Systems Thinking

With the exception of Epstein (1982, 1986), none of the cognitive theorists comprehended the need to integrate their approach with systems thinking. Treating couples requires more than doing Cognitive Therapy with two individuals in a room who happen to be married. Beck's (1988) recent book, *Love is Never Enough,* is a classic example of how an individualistic approach to treatment is applied to a system without a systemic perspective. A couple must always be understood as an interactional system. The cognitions within that system need to be conceptualized as part of an interactional, not just an individual system. Couples marry, stay together, and experience happiness and difficulties as a result of their shared cognitions.

There are two basic ways in which cognitions need to be conceptualized systemically. First, the couple may share many of the same, but irrational or unworkable ideas and cognitive distortions. These ideas may serve both to bind them together and to create dysfunctionality. For example, the couple may believe conflict should be avoided at all costs. The relationship serves to protect each of them from having to deal with anger and conflict. This idea binds the couple together, but it also creates a pathological condition in the relationship.

The second way in which cognitions can be understood systemically is in terms of their interlocking and complementary nature. The beliefs held by one may be complemented by the beliefs in the other. For example, one partner may think, "I must have my way," and the other may think, "I must be the perfect partner and let him or her do what she or he wants." Or a partner might think, "My partner is responsible for my moods," and the other partner may think, "I am responsible for my partner's happiness."

The cognitions must be processed within the context of the relationship as part of the interactional field. The impact of symmetrical and complementary cognitions can be discussed by each partner and the therapist. If one partner changes a cognition, what will the impact be on the other? How must the other change his or her thinking? How will the relationship be different? These questions require careful consideration in order to shift the focus from individual therapy to systems or couples therapy.

Techniques

EDUCATION

A significant part of a cognitive approach is teaching couples the basic principles of RET and Cognitive Therapy. The clinician may review the theory in the office and answer questions. It is essential that the partners understand the relationship between their cognitions *and* their feelings and actions. Until they believe changing their thinking will result in other change, therapy with this approach should not proceed. Bibliotherapy can also used to facilitate this learning process. The clinician may use handouts or recommend books that are easy to read such as, *Feeling Good* by David Burns (1980).

LEARNING TO SELF-MONITOR

The purpose of cognitive approaches is to help partners eventually identify their own individual and relational cognitive distortions and irrational thoughts. This process starts with education and is then worked on in the office. A technique to get the couple started is to ask them to answer the below questions at home and to bring their answers to the next session. Processing these answers may take several sessions.

As the process unfolds, the therapist carefully monitors the couple to help detect their distortions and negative statements. When a distortion is detected, it is fed back to the couple so they may begin to process it. As always, they should be asked to think the cognition through in accordance with the guidelines provided in the section on systems thinking. Specifically, does the other partner share the same or similar cognition or distortion or have one that is complementary? In other words, when a distortion or irrational thought is found for one partner, the therapist should work on developing a complete picture. The thought leads to a specific behavior. The behavior affects the other person, which means the other partner has a cognition about the behavior.

Once the thoughts of both partners are understood, it will then become clear what creates the problem. Both may then be asked to work on changing their thinking. After clearing up the irrational ideas and cognitive distortions, it is useful to obtain their thoughts about the relationship in general. The following questions may be asked to clarify this thinking:

1. What did you expect of marriage before you got married?
2. What did you expect of marriage just after you were married?
3. What do you expect of marriage now?

In addition, the couple may be asked to complete the following statements:

"A husband should _____." "A wife should _____."

The answers to these questions are then processed in the session. The couple would be asked to consider whether their thinking is realistic, productive, and workable. The clinician should not frame any of these thoughts as true or false or right or wrong. They can be framed as preferences, likes, or disbeliefs. This examination will help the partners to identify their distortions, enabling them to change their way of thinking. It is important to point out how the new thoughts will counter the old thoughts—but only with continued practice. Slips and regressions are to be expected.

The couple are reminded that old thoughts are deeply ingrained and automatic. By categorizing the commonly occurring distortions and irrational thoughts, the clients become more aware of when this type of thinking starts. Initially, it is useful to have clients do a daily review of what was discussed in the session in order to be more alert to the presence of problematic thinking.

This technique also involves becoming aware of all the negative cognitions associated with a specific problem. Once the negative cognitions have been made explicit, an attempt is made to change the cognition. The cognitions are either neutralized or changed in a positive direction. For example, if the problem is constant fighting, the underlying thought might be that the only way to preserve one's sense of self is to stay distant, with anger being used to create the needed distance.

Or a wife might complain that her husband doesn't tell her he loves her enough. The fact is that he rarely says anything. Her complaint is legitimate, but it is also escalated by her. She begins to think he does not love her and he is rejecting her by not saying something she has told him she would like. In this instance, it is important to change her cognition and, in turn, the behavior within the system. If she changes her thinking, then she might be nicer to him. He also needs to change his behavior by expressing more love and affection to her. His part of the problem could be that to tell his wife he loves her means he will be engulfed by her. His irrational thought might stem from a family of origin in which Mother was constantly manipulating the male partner for his approval and love. Once the husband can change his cognition, his attitude toward his wife will change and he will be freer to express his feelings.

OTHER TECHNIQUES

There are several other techniques that may be taught to the couple. Burns (1980) has identified 10 techniques in his book, two of which are particularly applicable to couples. The first is what he calls the *alternative interpretation method.* An event (A) can be interpreted in a number of ways. Negative interpretations are harmful to the relationship, while positive interpretations are helpful. Couples need to master the art of positively reframing each other's behaviors. The reframe should be believable and consistent with the facts.

For example, a couple may share the belief that intimacy is sharing all their time together. When one violates this assumption, a negative judgment is made. A positive frame would be that separateness and individuality are as much a part of intimacy as togetherness. Traits, characteristics, and attributes may all be given a positive frame with a little effort. The therapist should model positive reframing and then encourage the partners to look for new ways of thinking about each other. The more they stress the positive, the more they feel good.

The second technique is to *examine the evidence* for a particular thought. Do the facts point in only one direction? Are the facts even known? Assumptions by their nature are often not checked out or verified. The interpretation of an event may be made in-and-of oneself without regard for the other's input. Partners must learn to identify when they are making assumptions and then to keep an open mind until these assumptions are confirmed or disconfirmed. Assumptions may be so entrenched that the partner is only able to hear the voice in his or her head and not the input from the other person. When conversations become monologues, such that each keeps saying the same thing over and over, it is time for the partners to recognize that they are each captives of their own thinking. They need to turn attention outward in order to find out what the other person said.

CONCLUSION

Working with a couple means attending to their behavior, affect, and cognition. In the literature, emphasis on the cognitive aspect of the couple relationship has been lacking. This chapter stressed the usefulness of learning more about each partner's way of thinking and actual thoughts regarding the relationship. The essential point to remember from this chapter is that thoughts must be considered from a systemic frame of reference. The question is how the partners' thoughts form an interlocking system that leads to problems. Taken separately, the thoughts may seem acceptable. Considered together, the couple may be engaging in thoughts that put them at odds with or that place barriers to sharing greater intimacy. Just as with other issues, processing and changing the thoughts requires that the therapist go back and forth with the partners, thereby maintaining the balance. It is not a matter of a thought being right or wrong, but, rather, a question of whether the thinking is producing a workable relationship.

Chapter 13

Techniques of Marital Contracting

The purpose of this chapter is to discuss several techniques of marital contracting. A marital contract makes explicit those behaviors that are wanted in a marriage. The contract is usually written and identifies the behaviors to be exchanged in specific, concrete, and behavioral terms.

The use of contracts can be traced to the development of behavior therapy. According to L'Abate and McHenry (1983), five factors contributed to the development of contracting. First, as behavior therapy increased in use, behaviorists began to consider ways to use this approach with couples. The result was the development of behavioral marital therapy, with the emergence of several contractual approaches. Second, some therapists were becoming disillusioned with intrapsychic approaches. These approaches were not active and directive enough to deal with couple difficulties.

Third, as any field develops, it must produce reliable methods and demonstrate effectiveness. Contracting was a technique that could be scientifically replicated among clinicians. Fourth, the field of marital therapy needed to demonstrate that it produced the results claimed. Because contracting is replicable, it can be empirically evaluated for outcome. Finally, many couples coming for treatment were neither interested in or suitable for approaches that were cognitively or affectively oriented. These couples were primarily interested in changing the behaviors within the relationship.

The basic theory of marital contracts is that behavioral change leads to affective and cognitive change. It has been shown repeatedly that cognition and affect do follow from behavior. The basic purpose of a marital contract is to increase the number of positive exchanges in the relation-

171

ship. By increasing positive exchanges, the therapist is simultaneously decreasing punishing or coercive exchanges. Couples who are trapped in these negative exchanges are trying to get what they want and then retaliating when their needs are frustrated. Such a situation can create a power struggle in the relationship. Each partner attempts to "win" as a substitute for having his or her needs met.

Contracting is an ideal solution for obviating power struggles and creating positive exchanges. Because both partners contribute equally to the contract, they are creating a system of perceived equity and fairness. The contract or system they create diffuses the power struggle. With the power struggle being diffused, it is easier to begin making the positive changes specified in the contract.

The use of a contracting approach is more likely to work under certain conditions. First, both partners should be fully engaged in the therapeutic process. A contract cannot be developed by just one spouse. Both must be present and be working toward the same basic goal—to make the marriage fulfill their needs more effectively. Second, the partners must be relatively compliant, cooperative, and caring. If the couple are too angry, focused on externalizing or blaming each other, locked in a power struggle or impasse, this approach is not indicated. Third, each spouse must be willing to change his or her own behavior. They must both agree to try something different. Compromise is an important concept for the couple to comprehend. Each must know that by giving up something they value, they will gain other benefits.

Finally, the couple must be motivated to take control of their own relationship. A contract does not involve being told what to do, nor is it as mystical as just talking with a therapist who has charisma. The contract represents the couple's effort to take control of their own marriage in a way that appeals to common sense. Unconscious forces are not worked on directly. The personal commitment to change must be strong, and the therapist needs to reinforce each partner's individual change.

GENERAL PRINCIPALS OF CONTRACTING

Execute a Written Document

The term contract refers to a written agreement. A marital contract should also be placed in writing. Several reasons may be given to justify the need for a written contract. First, all important events in life are documented in writing. Birth certificates, death certificates, academic records, diplomas, all mark progress or events. The written word is permanent and has greater psychological import than the spoken word. It could be argued that the written word is more binding than the spoken word. Second, because the written word is permanent it is not easy to "forget" the agreement. Verbal statements may be ignored, repressed, confused, distorted, or otherwise minimized or sidetracked. A written record may be read and reread with the same meaning if it is clearly written. (Although written words can also have their meanings distorted until a mutually agreed upon interpretation of them is reached.)

Third, the fact that the message is permanent also allows the couple to use it as a constant reminder of their commitment. The contract may be displayed in some visible location or read daily as a reminder to help change the old habitual routine. Couples are usually asked to read the contract daily the first few weeks until it is committed to memory. Fourth, the contract should be carefully worded. Statements should be short, concise, and behavioral. The answer to the question of "who, does what, when, and how" should be clear for each behavioral exchange. Finally, the contract should be presented as an evolving document. The couple may renegotiate or modify items over time. The key point is that the couple have an agreement to deviate from rather than constantly working toward something that is never clear and explicit.

Be Realistic

The behaviors to be exchanged must be perceived as being fair and equitable. A contract that is perceived as being one-sided will only serve to generate more resentment and anger. The contract is designed to create equity and justice in the relationship. In order to create this sense of equity, both partners must be willing to make a contribution. These contributions may sometimes be felt as sacrifices for the greater good of the relationship. In its simplest form, the contract represents each partner's needs for giving and getting. What one partner wants to receive should be what the other ideally wants to give or, realistically, what the other is willing to give for the sake of reciprocity and marital satisfaction.

The behaviors to be exchanged must be under conscious control. One should not ask for that which the other cannot give or is unable to give.

For example, in one case a husband demanded his wife have sex with him to meet his requirements of equity and justice in the marriage. He agreed to give her friendship, which is what she wanted and he, in turn, expected her to give him sex. However, his wife was experiencing inhibited sexual desire and her ability to simply give him sex was thus impossible. He had to be educated regarding her present limitations in order for therapy to proceed on the basis of an exchange other than the one which he originally wanted.

Be Positive

The contract should avoid the use of punishment. Punishment involves withholding, taking away, and coercive acts. In order to formulate a positive emotional environment in the relationship, the contract needs to be worded as positively as possible, for example, "I want to give you," "I will do _____ for you," and "I agree to _____ ."

Be Inclusive

Many contracts we have seen specify only one behavior exchange. These contracts fail to address the complexity of a relationship. A couple may focus on one particular problem area, but this may not be the only change they desire. Additionally, if they fail at their one item contract, their contract fails. While it is much easier to develop a one-item contract, it is not advisable.

Developing the contract will require several sessions. The couple should be told the contract is not complete until they have all the items they believe to be important. By being inclusive rather than overfocused, more aspects of the couple's relationship come under scrutiny and more change occurs after implementation. This approach is consistent with the concept of first- versus second-order change. In second-order change the relationship itself changes, not just elements of the relationship.

Discuss Problems with Implementation

After the contract has been developed and the couple are ready to implement it, the therapist should take time to discuss ways in which the contract might not work. The couple is then asked to reread the contract in the session. Then the partners are asked to discuss ways they might fail to live up to their part. The partners are asked to speak only for self. The therapist may also add ideas that have emerged during previous discussions. The most common idea is that of the partner not living up to his or her side, which is viewed as making the contract null and void. Each partner needs to make a personal commitment to contribute 100 percent, irrespective of what the other partner does. The failure of a partner to fulfill his or her part will be addressed in the session following his or her failure to live up to the commitment.

Monitor Progress

An ingredient of contracting that is often underemphasized is that of monitoring progress. One interesting phenomenon that sometimes occurs with couples is that they begin to change, but do not "see" the change. In short, a lag may exist between the behavioral change and the perception of change. This phenomenon is consistent with evidence that suggests people are often more theory-driven than data-driven when monitoring events, that is, spouses may have a theory about how and why each one behaves. Often, new data are made to fit the theory or are discarded if they are not consistent with the theory. In one case a wife described her husband as incapable of having feelings. When he started to discuss his feelings in the couple's sessions, she dismissed his effort as an act designed to impress the therapist.

For systematic self-monitoring to occur each spouse must do a daily review of his or her progress. The question the partners should ask themselves is, "How am I doing?" To answer this question, the items on the contract are used as behavioral criteria. Each item is reviewed in order to assess whether it was fulfilled, the frequency with which it was done, and the satisfaction derived from fulfilling the item. This assessment leads to the development of an ongoing log, which is brought to the session where the therapist can monitor and reinforce the progress with the couple.

In the previous paragraph, a nonbehavioral assessment or subjective assessment was recommended, namely, the satisfaction derived from fulfilling the item. The contract is seen as providing equity in the relationship and helping each partner receive what she or he wants. Thus, it is rewarding. However, these rewards are not the only compensations available. Partners should be asked to reinforce each other when agreements are fulfilled. When partners notice one of the agreements being enacted, they need to express their appreciation. The act of expressing appreciation may be discussed in the session. Once it is clear the couple share this attitude, then the phrases used to express appreciation may be discussed. Discussing the phrasing is important because partners sometimes feel their spouse is being patronizing. The statements of appreciation create a positive reinforcement loop in the couple, further reinforcing the utility of the contract.

TECHNIQUES OF CONTRACTING

Three basic approaches to contracting may be found in the marital therapy literature. The first two to be discussed are derived from behavioral marital therapy and the third from a combination of therapeutic approaches.

Quid Pro Quo Contracts

This type of contract is one in which the behavioral exchanges are cross-linked (O'Leary & Turkewitz, 1978). Quid pro quo literally means "something for something." The partners agree that if one partner fulfills his or her agreement, then the other fulfills his or her agreement; the behaviors are contingent on each other. In order for this agreement to work, the behavior offered must be reinforcing to the other spouse. For example, George wants Mary to stop working at 3:00 P.M. on the dot and then together they will go to do something they both find enjoyable. Mary wants George to help her for two hours or to do two hours of chores each day of the weekend. They agree that if George does two hours of work, Mary will stop at 3:00 P.M. and they will do something enjoyable.

The Quid Pro Quo Contract has major problems. First, there is the question of who goes first. This issue should be settled in the session. It is important to define a behavioral cycle, that is, the period of time in which the two behaviors are linked. Within that cycle one partner may have the first turn. It may be they can alternate turns or that no one needs to be specified as going first. If one person does not meet the terms of the agreement, the other is under no obligation within the specified behavioral cycle.

When such a failure occurs, the couple should not respond to the event with anger, but with disappointment. One partner may note his or her disappointment. In contracting, the partners are advised to acknowledge anger in the other, but then to ignore it until the next session. If the anger is allowed, the couple get trapped once again in their cycle of blaming and counterblaming. In the session the anger may be explored as a block to prevent change, as a hidden agenda, and so on (see Chapter 11 on Conflict Resolution). The fact that a behavioral cycle has been defined allows the partners an opportunity to try to fulfill the agreement during the next cycle. If the cycle is day-by-day, then a new cycle and new opportunity would be available each day. Having short behavioral cycles enhances the chances for successful interaction during the week. Thus, the couple should be encouraged to think of daily exchanges.

Good Faith Contracts

Weiss, Hops, and Patterson (1973) introduced this type of contract. Unlike the Quid Pro Quo Contract, this technique does not tie together or make contingent the partner's behaviors. Each partner makes a commitment in good faith to provide the other with particular behaviors. If the discussed behavior is given, the person receives a reward that is independent of the partner's behavior. For example, if a husband wants his wife to go biking with him on Saturday and his wife goes with him, she chooses a reward she would like, such as going out one evening during the week with her friends. Good Faith Contracts are easy to formulate when the number of behaviors is small. However, as the contract grows, the number of reinforcements becomes more and more difficult to find.

A variation of the Good Faith Contract is to ask the partners to help each other without any extrinsic reward. The reward would be the intrinsic satisfaction experienced from the improved and happier relationship. We employ this technique frequently because it is simple and agreeable to most couples. When using this technique it is very useful to have the partners verbally reward each other as was pointed out earlier.

Covenant Contracts

This method of contracting was developed by Clifford Sager (1976). It is different from behavioral contracts because of its much broader form. Emotions as well as behaviors are included in this contract. To use Sager's approach it is necessary to understand two components of his theory.

Sager (1976) stated that all couples have an implicit and explicit interactional contract, which determines the behavior of each spouse within the relationship. The individual contracts may be conscious and verbalized, conscious and nonverbalized, or unconscious and nonverbalized. It is clear from this theory that much of what determines the behavior within a relationship is not known to the partners. The contract is implicit and unconcious. One of the purposes of covenant contracting is to make those nonverbalized and unconscious expectations known to oneself and one's partner.

As the couple become clearer about their unconscious contract they may find three types of situations. Their contracts may be congruent. A congruent contract is based on healthy needs and emphasizes a trading off of needs, wants, and desires. A second possibility is the complementary contract. In this case the partners use the traits of the other to complete some missing part in self. For example, a shy person might use the extroversion of her or his mate to compensate for his or her deficiency. A third possibility is the conflictual contract. This contract makes effective and rewarding interactions impossible. Unfortunately, much of this conflicted material is unconscious and gradually emerges in the relationship. A couple might marry knowing some problems exist, but not the full extent of the problems.

The Covenant Contract involves making the implicit and unspoken expectations explicit. For example, a woman who feels that her husband will leave her when he becomes angry—because of her history of having partners who had actually done so—might need her husband to reassure her or affirm his commitment during or after a fight. Assessment and treatment are viewed as inseparable dialectic processes. The process of making the expectations explicit is diagnostic and also therapeutic in that the expectations may be changed or renegotiated.

In doing this type of contract each partner is asked to address four sets of issues: self, marriage, spouse, and children. For each issue a want list is constructed. In addition to these four sets of issues, Sager (1976) has developed lists of questions that help to stimulate thinking about different aspects of the marriage. These questions are given to the couple early in the process so the partners may have time to consider their answers. Following each partner's reading of his or her list, the therapist helps the couple determine what is realistic and what can be negotiated. The process of doing the Covenant Contract may be fairly specific in format. Once the expectations are explicit, the therapist may choose to proceed in a less structured way.

Of the three types of contracts described, covenant contracting is the most complex and time consuming. The therapist assumes there are unconscious expectations. Time is needed to help the partners become aware that such expectations exist; giving them the questions to consider helps to raise their unconscious expectations into awareness. Educating the partners that such expectations exist and giving them the questions to consider help to raise their awareness. The process of therapy itself promotes self-awareness, allowing for the emergence of unconscious expectations.

However, not all of these expectations will become apparent to the partners. As the therapist gets to know how the couple relate, especially in conflictual ways, these expectations can be inferred by the therapist. Once an inference is made, the therapist may suggest to the couple that such an expectation exists. Additional inferences can be drawn from genogram information. Patterns, messages, and other key family-of-origin experiences tend to create specific expectations.

In one case a wife complained that she wanted her husband to be able to listen to and understand her, yet she said he had *never* been able to do so. The fact was that when he did understand her, it either did not register or did not count because she said it was about something trivial. Her behavior suggested she expected her husband would never have the qualities needed to listen to her. In her family of origin she felt the same way, that is, no one cared enough about her to listen. In spite of the fact that this woman said she wanted understanding, she was the one who could not allow it to occur and she was unconsciously sabotaging herself. When confronted about this pattern, she denied that such a thing was possible.

The problem for the therapist is that when some of these expectations are discovered, it can be difficult to get the client to accept them. Such a client would need gentle yet persistent confrontation over time. This task is best accomplished through enactments in the office. In the case above, the wife would be asked to state what she needed, her husband encouraged and taught to respond, and her reaction noted. When she begins to discount his ability or sincerity, she should be confronted. Video playback in the session might be useful also to help her see the way she refuses to acknowledge her husband's attempts to communicate with her.

CONCLUSION

The three techniques of contracting described in this chapter represent varying types of behavioral approaches. There exists ample evidence to suggest changing behavior eventually leads to changes in affect and cognition. The therapist's choice is whether to focus on behavior, cognition, or affect from the outset. A behavioral approach utilizing a contract is useful with concrete, less verbal, and less psychologically sophisticated couples. There also must be sufficient motivation to change. In addition, the therapist should offer ample praise to help facilitate the changes and to stand as an all-important model for the couple.

When the partners see the therapist being positive and offering praise, they may begin to internalize that behavior as part of their own. Approaching one another positively further invites change from the other, which, in turn, creates even more positive behavior exchanges.

Chapter 14

Feelings

In individual psychotherapy there are approaches to treatment devoted solely to affect or emotion. Gestalt Therapy, for example, has been a major force in psychotherapy and deals exclusively with emotional awareness and expression. However, marital therapies have devoted little attention to the role of feelings in therapy. In fact, in some major approaches such as paradoxical, strategic, and behavioral, feelings are viewed as a hindrance to effective therapeutic work. Proponents of these approaches often speak of the need to avoid dealing with feelings because they are seen as a distraction. Of all the major approaches to systems/marital therapy, not one gives serious attention to the role of feelings (Gurman & Kniskern, 1981b), despite the fact that marriage is fundamentally an emotional attachment.

Although strong unconscious forces may exist, couples enter relationships on a voluntary basis and form the relationship on the basis of one overtly stated feeling—*love*. Close relationships such as marriage frequently evoke the strongest emotions an individual ever experiences. Rage, anger, and hatred may be felt in shocking intensity. Close relationships can also distort perceptions and feelings. During the idealization stage of courtship, partners may be "intoxicated" with feelings of love to the point of overlooking other feelings they have toward the partner and significant problems that might deter marriage. In an effort to sustain a close relationship, other feelings might be ignored, denied, suppressed, or repressed. For example, a partner who fears anger might suppress it in order to avoid harming or losing the other partner.

The role emotions play in a relationship is obviously complex and not predictable until the partners are understood. The nature of emotions themselves is not clear. Several theories are available to define and explain them and were recently reviewed by Greenberg and Johnson (1986a) in an article on the use of affect in marital therapy.

The purpose of this chapter is to discuss some techniques that are helpful in facilitating the use of emotions with couples. We will avoid theoretical and academic explorations in favor of the practical.

EXPECTATIONS AND FEELINGS

In the chapter on cognitive therapy the relationship between cognition and feeling was described. Basically, feelings are determined by the cognitions. In a close relationship a number of strong and stable expectations come into play. When these expectations are met, partners feel satisfied, happy, fulfilled, gratified, contented, respected, cared for, and loved. On the other hand, when expectations are not met or are in conflict, other less pleasant emotions emerge. These feelings are an indication that expectations are not meshing. The therapist may wish to focus on a feeling to understand what is being felt and to validate the feeling and then move on to uncover expectation on which it is based. In some cases, the expectation is unknown to the partner. The only indication of its existence is its emotional effect. The feeling is much like the devastation resulting from a storm. One cannot see the wind, only its effects. Giving the feeling reality serves to give heretofore unknown expectations authenticity.

PROMOTING AWARENESS OF FEELINGS

Unfortunately, some marital therapists have dealt with the issues of feelings in an oversimplified way. The therapist has simply asked, "How do you feel?" The client responds and then the issue must be dropped until the therapist asks the question again. Apparently the therapist believes that ventilation of the feeling alone is enough. Working with feelings always involves two steps. The first is to help the person to be aware of the feeling, and the second is to help the person express the feeling.

One of our colleagues, Larry Hof (Hof & Miller, 1981), has developed an exercise to help with both of these aspects. He calls this exercise the "World of Feelings." This exercise is used with couples who are having some trouble getting in touch with their feelings and are not at the extremes of being suppressed or angry. The exercise is described below. The first part consists of instructions for the partners followed by a couple's exercise. This exercise was designed to be done at home in roughly one hour.

My World of Feelings Experience*

15 Minutes 1. Personal Reading: "The World of Feelings"

15 Minutes 2. Individuals complete statements on "My World of Feelings" form.

20 Minutes 3. Couples sit facing each other, knees touching, and decide who will start.

4. The person starting says, "In our marriage, when we relate together, I am happiest when. . . ." Having completed the statement, the person maintains eye contact as much as possible.

5. Partner is to listen attentively to the feelings being expressed, and to accept them. The only comment acceptable is a question for clarification of what the person means. Statements are not to be discussed nor disagreed with. Hear them, accept them, receive them as a gift of the one person to the other.

6. After the first person has shared her/his response to item number 1, the partner then shares her/his response to the same item.

7. Repeat the process until all the items have been completed.

10 Minutes 8. Talk together with your partner about what you experienced, thought, and felt as you went through this experience. Discuss the value of this experience for you and for your relationship.

* This technique was developed by Larry Hof and appears in Hof and Miller's *Marriage Enrichment*, pp. 96–98. Copyright © 1981. Reprinted with permission.

The World of Feelings

The world of feelings is the world of affection and sentiment, the world of emotion and passion. It is the world of happiness and sadness, of joy and anger, of excitement and boredom. My feelings are my spontaneous emotional responses to the events that occur in the world around me, the emotional responses associated with, and triggered by, my fulfilled or unfulfilled expectations, and my interpretations of events and behaviors. My feelings are expressed in and through my body; I may speak faster and louder when I am excited, and slower and softer when I am sad; my body may shake when I laugh, and my eyes may fill with tears when I am in pain. Even when I am not consciously aware of my feelings, my body is frequently giving off clues that I am feeling something, clues that other people may sense.

During any given day, I will feel a variety of feelings:

Happiness	Confusion	Relief
Satisfaction	Sadness	Loneliness
Hope	Boredom	Joy
Apathy	Fear	Love
Pain	Anger	Confidence
Suspense	Suspicion	Remorse
Silliness	Contentment	Pride
Irritation	Peacefulness	Tiredness
Hopelessness	Anticipation	Reverence
Surprise		

The list could be expanded almost endlessly, with subtle variations and differing degrees of each feeling being present at different times. I can feel several feelings at once, and those feelings can conflict with each other.

My feelings are a very real and valuable part of me. They are just as important as my thoughts, my senses, and my behaviors. They can help me to deepen my understanding of life and the impact of people and events upon me. My joy helps me to celebrate and to identify things and people I like. My boredom gives me clues that I would rather be doing something else. My fears help me to protect myself. Without my feelings, I would live a greatly impoverished life.

Yet, for some reason, many of us have been taught to disregard our feelings— all of them, or a select few "bad" feelings. Some people have been taught to be "rational." Some have been taught to deny or avoid anger, pain, pride, or sexual feelings. Perhaps, each of us has a little list that we keep inside of "acceptable" and "unacceptable" feelings. Others feel them internally, but we don't permit ourselves to express them without words or actions. For example, we want to avoid conflict, so we don't express our anger. We don't want to be "soft," so we withhold our warmth. We don't want to appear "weak," so we don't disclose our fears.

If my feelings are to serve me and help me make sense of life, I must be aware of them and their heights and depths, and be able to express them appropriately in words and actions. If I deny or avoid them, I lose the ability to control them and they can gain control of me. Then, they may emerge when I don't want them to, perhaps inappropriately. Or, they may literally "eat a hole in my stomach" or "give me a pounding headache." In some way, I pay a great price when I refuse to let my feelings have an appropriate and natural place in my life.

When I accept the fact that it is normal to feel a whole range of feelings,

I am freed from justifying my feelings or apologizing for them. I simply recognize that, "I am human; therefore, I feel. You are human; therefore, you feel, too." As I accept that fact, and increase my awareness of my feelings, I can express them in many ways. The choice of how I will express them is mine to make. I can change old ways of expressing them. The more I practice, the more I will become used to expressing my feelings.

In a marital relationship, the ability of two individuals to be aware of the whole range of feelings, to express them appropriately, and to accept them in themselves and in each other can pave the way for increased self-awareness and for stronger bonds of trust and deeper intimacy. It may make each partner more vulnerable, too. But, perhaps the potential for self-awareness and growth, and for increased trust and intimacy, is worth the risk!

My World of Feelings

Please complete the following statements:

1. In our marriage, when we relate together, I am happiest when. . . .
2. In our marriage, when we relate together, I am saddest when. . . .
3. In our marriage, when we relate together, I am angriest when. . . .
4. The best thing about our marriage is. . . .
5. I feel most afraid when. . . .
6. I feel loved when you. . . .
7. My greatest concern/fear for our marriage is. . . .
8. What I like most about myself is. . . .
9. What I dislike most about myself is. . . .
10. What I like most about you is. . . .
11. My greatest concern/fear for you is. . . .
12. The feelings that I have the most difficulty sharing with you are. . . .
13. The feelings that I can share most easily with you are. . . .
14. Right now I feel . . . towards you.
15. Right now I feel . . . towards myself.
16. I feel . . . sharing these feelings with you.

GETTING IN TOUCH

As we indicated earlier, some partners are more emotionally repressed than others. For those partners more work is needed. They are asked to define a feeling and to keep a feeling diary. Partners are first asked to define a feeling because they often confuse thoughts, judgments, and feelings. They must learn how to differentiate these by questioning themselves and by getting assistance from the therapist and, in many cases, from their partner. The type of confusion one commonly comes across is exemplified by the client who says, "I feel (good), (bad), (okay), etc." Just because the word "feel" is used in the sentence, does not mean a feeling is being defined. This example involves value statements or judgments. The partner could have said, "I feel happy, unhappy, contented." These terms represent feelings.

The daily diary is reviewed weekly. The partners are asked to note their feelings and the triggers for those feelings. Furthermore, they are asked to let the feelings "register" by staying with them for a few minutes. For some people feelings are fleeting. As a consequence, the feeling is not registered or discussed later with one's partner.

The second half of this exercise involves the partner choosing one or two feelings to share with the other person. Time is to be set aside in the evening for this activity. The other partner should reflect back the feeling and discuss it with the partner who shared it. These exercises are simple homework for the couple who need straightforward emotional assistance. Many couples need much more.

FILTERING EMOTIONS

One of the most common problems in couples is that they filter all their emotions through one emotional channel—the most usual of which is anger. In other words, all the emotions experienced are either experienced and/or expressed in anger. A partner may experience guilt, fear, hurt, depression, insecurity, and so on, yet express any one of these emotions as anger. Anger becomes a defense to protect the partner from having to deal with an emotion she or he is ill-equipped to handle.

When the therapist observes one emotion being used to cover up others, it is time to explore the other underlying feelings. It is usually not difficult to guess what those feelings are likely to be. Continued explorations, with the client beginning to attend to and express the underlying feeling, are helpful.

The problem, of course, with revealing and expressing the underlying feeling is what the partner believes will happen if she or he does so. Once the unexpressed feelings have been identified, the partners may be asked what makes their expression so difficult. They may believe the partner will not hear them or will use the feelings against them. This belief can be processed objectively by the therapist, checked out with the partner, and then an enactment can take place in the session in which the couple deal with the feelings while being coached by the therapist.

GENOGRAMS AND FEELINGS

When a partner believes certain feelings should not be felt and/or expressed, genogram work may help to uncover the reason. Questions about how feelings were handled in the family, which feelings were acceptable, not acceptable, and how different feelings were expressed elucidate the historical basis of the problem. The partner can then begin to see how certain feelings were always blocked.

The Feelings Genogram may be used to collect considerable information about feelings in the family. Some questions the therapist may ask include the following.

FEELINGS GENOGRAM

1. What were the dominant feelings for each member of your family?
2. What was the predominant feeling in your family? Who set the mood?
3. Which feelings were expressed most often, most intensely?
4. Which feelings were not allowed? How were members punished when an unallowed feeling was expressed?
5. What happened to the unexpressed feelings in the family?
6. Who knew/did not know about how others felt?
7. What happened to you when you expressed the taboo feeling?
8. How did you learn how to deal with these so-called unacceptable feelings?
9. Did others try to tell you how you should feel?
10. Did you ever see anyone lose control over his or her feelings?
11. Do you find yourself having feelings you can't explain, but are close to feelings you had in the past?

In one case a man was a "pseudospouse" to his mother. He learned that his mother desperately needed his love and admiration. He eventually discovered that by always being cheerful and loving he could win mother's approval. In his marriage he gave the appearance of all being well emotionally, while he was seething with frustration, anger, and resentment. The emotions in this case were in fact directed toward his mother, but were being displaced onto his wife.

When the emotions of the partners are not consistent with the situation, it is useful to think about emotional displacement from the family of origin. In one extreme case, a husband always found reason to be critical and angry toward his wife. Genogram exploration revealed he was carrying unresolved anger toward his parents. Conversely, his wife had felt guilt and depression for many years. She was the peacemaker in her own family, yet she was told she had failed in this role. She was unconsciously compelled to keep trying until everyone felt happy again.

EMOTIONAL CONGRUENCE

Much of what has been discussed up to now assumes the feeling is what it appears to be. However, feelings may also be distorted or absent. The therapist's use of self is the only way to comprehend these two situations. As the therapist listens and resonates to the clients' situations emotionally, she or he may notice a lack of affect or an affect that does not quite fit. Asking a question about feelings is most appropriate at this time. If the partner does not identify the feeling, the therapist may give the client time to safely explore the question, ask questions to guide the client, or supply the missing affect. The therapist could say, "If I were in your place . . ." or "I can't imagine you didn't feel. . . ." If the client agrees with the emotion, the therapist detects that the therapy is on track. Once the feeling has been identified more exploration can be done. The therapist may want to know what it means to feel". . . ," whether the person has felt that way before, what made it so hard to identify the feeling, and what she or he fears about expressing it. During this exploration, the partner is kept actively involved. Obviously, one partner is sharing this information with his or her mate, and the other partner reflects the feeling back and may be asked to discuss how she or he deals with the feelings in question, too.

In one case a woman became very upset and started to cry when her partner told her he did not want her to make love to him when she was not interested. In the early part of this relationship the woman had frequently had sex with him when she did not feel the desire. On the surface his statement should have made her feel accepted and respected. However, her response was actually a distortion, because she could not allow herself to believe him. Her father and first husband were both narcissistic individuals who were only interested in meeting their own needs. When she started to hear her partner take care of her, she was reminded of the emotional betrayal and abandonment of the previous men in her life, and this reminder provoked her tears.

MANAGING INAPPROPRIATE AND INTENSE AFFECT

Just as with all other issues that emerge during the therapy hour, the therapist has a responsibility to provide an emotionally safe environment for both partners. When anger is being expressed through inappropriate behaviors such as snide remarks, critical remarks, shouting, or demanding, the therapist can intervene to establish some rules about what is *appropriate behavior.* The partner would then be asked to discuss the feelings behind those behaviors in a more constructive or assertive way. Many partners will have no idea about alternative modes of expression. The therapist may coach the partner through or model the expression of the feeling. The partner who is helped to express the feeling assertively allows the other partner to reflect back this feeling. The other partner may have equal difficulty in reflecting the feeling. They may have problems in hearing certain feelings whether they are appropriately or inappropriately expressed.

When affect is too intense the therapist needs to cool the session down. The therapist can accomplish this task by slowing down the pace. Usually the couple heat up emotionally when they talk directly to each other. The therapist can take a much more assertive role diffusing the couple's interaction by asking the couple to address the therapist, not each other. Additionally, the therapist can ask questions that are factually oriented. Asking about who does what, in what sequence, takes the partners away from their immediate feelings and directs them to take a more detached perspective.

INTENSIFYING AFFECT

Conversely, if the therapist wants to intensify affect, it is essential to promote talking and to focus on the partner's implicit or explicit feelings. This technique basically involves asking a couple to enact a problem. They are directed to discuss some problem that is known to be emotionally laden. As they discuss the problem, the therapist asks the partners to talk specifically about feelings. When feelings are not expressed directly, but are detected or inferred by the therapist, the process may be interrupted so the therapist can draw out the feeling. When the feeling(s) has been sufficiently amplified, the therapist directs the couple to continue their dialogue.

In one case a wife felt her husband's parents were too intrusive. When she brought the issue up, she made a statement that they spent too much time at their house. The therapist had her talk about how she felt, and went back and forth with the partners. Fifteen minutes later, the wife took a strong stand realizing just how distressed and resentful she was about the situation. The therapist kept encouraging her to let herself feel those feelings which her husband said were "not true." He did not like the fact that she was resentful, but he understood the consequences of her feelings in terms of the marriage.

CONCLUSION

The therapist has the task of controlling feelings in the session. This task involves intensifying affect where necessary, changing the mode of expression when inappropriate, and facilitating a controlled release over time when the affect would otherwise run away.

Bringing feelings into marital therapy can add a dimension of humanness and connection among all parties not experienced in other approaches. At first, it may be frightening because the couple covertly communicate their fear of feelings. Once this fear has been challenged, the couple feel stronger and the therapist experiences a unique emotional bond with them.

Chapter 15

Extending Techniques from the Office to Home Using Homework

with Marian Brooks, M.S.

The value of out-of-session behavioral tasks in marital therapy has been recognized for several decades (Sheldon & Ackerman 1974). Interpretation, analysis, and reflection, while integral parts of individual therapy, are insufficient in and of themselves as means of implementing solutions to the day-to-day problems faced by most couples and families. According to L'Abate (1986) and Andolfi (1980) the therapist must play an active and directive role both during the clinical hour and in the delegation of assignments at home. Clients learn by doing and so need the opportunity to practice repeatedly new behaviors and to process their results in order to develop alternative, more functional attitudes, cognitions, behaviors, and feelings.

Much that has been written on the subject of homework in psychotherapy is vague and confusing. Authors contradict each other and research results are variable and limited. Tasks are often geared to the theoretical framework of the many and varied models of marital and family therapy, rather than more generally applicable. Step-by-step, how-to directives on this subject are hard to come by.

Sheldon and Ackerman (1974) were pioneers in stressing the importance of homework assignments in enhancing desired behavior change through education and skill building. Their book was individually focused and was the first to design tasks to match specific difficulties. The authors discussed the importance of establishing rapport between client and therapist to promote compliance and emphasized the development of a clear understanding of problems and goals. Homework, they stated, must be clear and manageable, its logic explained, and the work reviewed in the next session. When tasks were not completed, the reasons for non-

191

compliance must be explored carefully. Clients were told what to do, how often to do it, to record the results, and to bring them to the next session. Sometimes the scheduling of the next appointment was contingent upon completion of the assignment. These assignments and tasks, however, were addressed to the individual and his or her problem area.

Warburton and Alexander (1985) focused on the establishment of the credibility of the therapist, a detailed assessment process, clarity and specificity in assigning tasks, and the utilization of methods to deal with resistance. Once again strategies and assignments were individually designed.

According to Strong and Claiborn (1982), compliance is enhanced when clients understand the rationale in following the therapist's directives, when they perceive that there is a choice in carrying out the homework, and when instructions are implicit rather than explicit. Change occurs more readily when viewed as an emergence of what is already within the individual and as growth in his or her personal power and control. The complex needs and responses of couples and families were not taken into account.

More specific to families, Aponte and Van Deusen (1981) regarded task setting as a means of redirecting dysfunctional interactional patterns in families. Such tasks were used as vehicles for establishing appropriate boundaries, alliances, and hierarchies. Minuchin (1974) also suggested a variety of restructuring interventions along similar lines. Such interventions were the outgrowth of a school of thought rather than a reflection of the unique problems and goals of each couple or family.

Bowenian therapists (Bowen, 1978) use homework to teach or coach individuals in reconstructing relationships with members of their families of origin in a healthier way in order to develop a more differentiated self. Tasks outside of sessions are designed with this goal in mind rather than simultaneously addressing couple/family interaction directly (e.g., a wife might be instructed in how to resolve an old conflict with her father that was getting reenacted with her husband).

Social learning theorists like Jacobson (1981) and Stuart (1980) proposed that the utilization of positive reinforcement, behavioral exchange contracts, problem-solving, conflict resolution, and communication training are the foundations of successful marital relationships. The importance of pretreatment assessment in the office and at home, the development of a collaborative effort, and the explanation of the treatment and its relevance to mutually agreed-upon goals were highlighted. Resistance was seen as an expression of ambivalence and as a reaction to the difficulty of change, rather than as a desire to maintain the status quo. "Inducing" a collaborative set and "skillfully implementing" treatment strategies, however, were left to the therapist's ingenuity or trial-and-error efforts. The role of the symptom, the history of each individual, the couple, the family, and the impact of other stressors are, for the most part, ignored by the behavioral therapist in designing homework assignments that address significant problems on several levels at once.

In contrast, a strategic marital/family therapist will often delegate homework tasks without explanation, be indirect, reframe, restrain change, and even prescribe the symptom in order to "outwit the resistance" (Weeks & L'Abate, 1982). Here, although the function of the symptom is well understood, skill building and education are underplayed.

In a recent book, L'Abate (1986) described the use of systematic homework assignments (SHWAs). These assignments are the vehicle through which his systematic family therapy approach is actually implemented. There are two basic issues in this approach—negotiation and intimacy. These two issues are broken down still further into specific elements that are systematically organized for the family to work through at home. But working through these issues is usually not discussed openly. This process facilitates treatment and should help to reduce the time spent in the office.

The literature on tasks, assignments, and homework leaves the therapist with considerable confusion about what to do and how to do it. How does he or she have directives flow from the session and from the interaction between therapist and clients? How does the therapist create a customized fit between the partners' history, capacity, and commitment to work as a unit toward desired goals *and* the step-by-step process used to attain these goals? Exactly how does the therapist enhance compliance, deal with resistance, and learn from failure?

TYPES OF HOMEWORK

There are basically two types of homework assignments. The first type of homework is designed to provide information that promotes awareness, challenges attitudes, and supplies the tools necessary to establish new skills. This type of homework is known as *Bibliotherapy*. A number of self-help books are currently available which may be prescribed. These books should be used exclusively with those clients who are motivated to read and to discuss the material.

The second type of homework is task-oriented and is designed to change behavior. These tasks may be paradoxical or linear (Weeks & L'Abate, 1982). Paradoxical tasks are those that seem contrary to common sense and produce quantum leaps in behavior change. Linear tasks are those that change behavior in a systematic, step-wise fashion. The assumption is that behavior may be shaped slowly over a period of time, given the proper conditions and appropriate experiences. In short, the client-system changes by doing.

Examples of linear homework have been widely discussed in family therapy (Nichols, 1984). The problem is that very little has been written on how to actually give homework. Assigning homework is a complex process involving knowing how and what to suggest, being able to facilitate compliance, and dealing with resistance. One of the most common errors new therapists make is to prescribe homework because it is "the thing to do" without actually understanding the process. In these cases, the homework is usually an idea gleaned from the professional literature, or perhaps a case study, and may not be appropriate or relevant to the couple or individual being treated.

CREATING HOMEWORK ASSIGNMENTS

The content of the homework assignment should emerge organically from the session. The homework should not simply be assigned to the client at the end of a session. Creating a homework assignment is best achieved through collaboration with the client. During the session the therapist and client-system are working toward a specific (behavioral) change. The question is how to bring about the change. When the clients have a clear definition of the desired change, they can then become participants in the collaborative process of creating homework to achieve that end. The therapist asks what type of change is wanted and how the client-system envisions this change being facilitated outside the session.

The change to be created should be approached systematically. Goals must be broken down into small steps from simple to complex, from less threatening to more threatening, and from more behavioral to more affective. The homework also should be congruent with the clients' style of learning. Some clients respond best when mechanical or highly structured assignments are developed. Others need experiences that are basically unstructured and promote creative engagement.

Whatever the homework is to be, under no circumstances should an assignment be prescribed that isn't first practiced in the session. In addition, the client-system should demonstrate that it possesses the motivation and fundamental skills to continue practicing it at home.

To ask clients to perform a homework task without having first demonstrated readiness is setting the client-system up for failure. One of the purposes of homework is to provide successful experiences, which in turn promote a greater sense of accomplishment, achievement, hope, and a spirit of cooperation for those involved. It also counters the emerging sense of learned helplessness, which begins to occur after a series of perceived failures in the client-system.

The issue of commitment and responsibility is important in starting the process of carrying out the homework. The therapist needs to ask each member of the client-system to make a commitment to carry out his or her part of the work. Commitment is a critical factor in whether homework is completed and in the success of therapy generally. By asking each partner to make a personal commitment, responsibility remains clearly within each individual for his or her failure or success. In many cases, a member of the system will wait for his or her partner to initiate the homework and then blame the other for noncompliance. When discussing commitment, the therapist should include how each person deals with his or her own resistance (e.g., How will you fail to get this done in spite of your good intentions now?) and with the resistance of his or her partner.

STRUCTURAL ELEMENTS

The homework itself has several structural elements. These elements are time, duration, frequency, and place (T, D, F, P). The task should be carried out at a particular time of day, protected from interference. In the session the couple should discuss when they can schedule the task and what each/both need to do to avoid any intrusions. This discussion has the effect of giving the task, hence the relationship, priority.

The duration of the task refers to how long the client-system stays engaged around the assignment. A common error is to prescribe a task that is too long or too complicated. For example, many couples cannot tolerate more than a few minutes of talking with each other. Asking a couple to talk 30 minutes to one hour is impossible for most couples in the beginning phase of therapy.

The third element is frequency, How many times during the day/week is the assignment to be done? Again, the therapist needs to take a conservative approach at the beginning of treatment. For example, a couple might be able to manage three, 10-minute circumscribed talks during a week.

The final element is place. In order to change old habits, new associations are helpful. Couples who have argued intensely in the bedroom or living room need to change location for talking. A location that is comfortable and free of distraction and old destructive associations is preferable.

At some point in the session the therapist should discuss the importance of practice and the usefulness of even small changes. Clients often overestimate the gains to be made from homework, and underestimate the effort required to make such gains. One of this author's favorite sayings is "practice, practice, and more practice." Sometimes it helps to talk about how long and how much practice is involved in learning such things as tennis, golf, proper grammar, and so on.

The therapist should point out to the clients that homework is always a no-lose proposition. If the homework is done and the outcome is good, then the goal has been achieved. If the homework is not done or a good outcome is not achieved, then more data have been obtained. Because this information was generated in a context created during the therapeutic process, it is usually easier to understand the factors contributing to success or failure. In a sense, homework is an experiment. Regardless of the results, everyone learns something.

At the end of the session, the assignment should be repeated to make sure everyone is clear about what is to be done. Some clients benefit by taking notes. The therapist should also record the assignment in detail in order to follow up at the the next session.

The therapist will communicate disinterest in the homework by forgetting it altogether or by failing to follow up at the beginning of the next session. If the homework is done, whether successfully or unsuccessfully, the client-system should be praised. It is natural to praise clients who are successful. Clients who attempt but fail can still be commended for their effort and for taking responsibility (making sure that the therapist's comments are devoid of real or implied sarcasm). Then, the entire experience is evaluated in order to extract as much information as possible about the positive and negative outcome.

In the case of a successful experience, another assignment is then created which builds on the first. A failed assignment may be reassigned once obstacles have been examined and removed or a different assignment may be developed. The processing of resistance will be more fully addressed in the last section of this chapter.

EXAMPLES OF HOMEWORK ASSIGNMENTS

The tasks that follow, when properly selected and delivered to couples in treatment, can address problems on several different levels simultaneously.

1. Communication is one of the most common problems couples bring to therapists. Having each member of a couple talk for five minutes about him or herself on a nonconflictual topic while his or her partner simply listens and reflects is an effective task for building the foundation of empathetic listening and constructive problem solving. The couple need to set aside 10 minutes (five for each) free from distraction several times a week to practice this skill. They first perform this task during the therapy hour so that the clinician can coach the couple through the process. The clients decide how often, when, where, and how long they can realistically complete this assignment, and whether or not it addresses their target areas for change. They discuss what might interfere with task completion.

The performance of the task requires some (albeit short) period of time when the relationship is a priority, promotes some level of intimacy, and decreases the amount of projection between the pair. It may realign hierarchies and detriangulate unhealthy alliances. Performance of the task can be diagnostic of the nature of the commitment between partners and to the therapeutic process. If the assignment is completed successfully, the therapist explores in detail feelings, thoughts, and behaviors and builds upon the earlier foundation with the clients' input. However, if the task has failed in some way, or has not even been attempted, the task may be repeated, perhaps in smaller steps or redesigned. The couple are asked what would enable them to carry out the assignment and what concerns they might have if the exercise, in fact, leads to the solution of the problem.

2. Having each member of a couple complete and share a genogram assists partners in learning how the patterns of the past are being acted out in their current struggles with each other in the present. Awareness of one's own and one's partner's history promotes greater empathy and less reactivity as well as the possibilities of alternative ways of perceiving, feeling, and acting in a given situation. For example, knowledge about a parent's lack of concern for a child, now an adult, can help that person and his or her spouse understand the confusing desire for and yet the rejection of affection and approval. As a result, the ambivalent behavior feels somewhat less like a personal affront to the person on the receiving end of the anger and hurt.

Furthermore, discussion allows for less realistic expectations on the part of the person who unconsciously yearns for his or her partner to make up for all the wounds of the past. The task addresses the issues of expectations and communication on psychodynamic, cognitive, and affective levels. It brings the past into the present in a useful way. In sessions, the clinician guides the couple through the process, taking detours where necessary, but directing them back to the main highway. Between office visits, clients are instructed to gather information about parents, grandparents, aunts, uncles, and other relatives, setting in motion the process of change in perception, feelings, and patterns of behavior with individuals outside of but influencing the couple dyad.

3. Suggesting that couples spend the week noticing the positive in the relationship and in each other can reverse the negative momentum which has probably been escalating for some time prior to treatment. Each partner is instructed not to discuss the findings but to bring a list to the next session. If the task has been completed, clients build on and process its success. If not, the assignment may be repeated or altered. Impediments to progress are removed and fears about success examined.

PROMOTING COMPLIANCE TO HOMEWORK

Strong and Claiborn (1982) discussed three principles that are useful in increasing spontaneous compliance. These principles should be particularly useful when resistance is high and the clients do not believe they have control over their behavior. The first principle is choice. It is important to give the prescription in such a way that the client perceives choice in how to respond. Common techniques include asking the client to think of alternatives, asking focused questions which lead the client in certain directions, and providing latitude for what the client does. The use of language is important in creating a sense of choice. The therapist should avoid terms that have a polarizing and/or perjorative effect. Absolutes such as right versus wrong, good versus bad, sane versus crazy, and truth versus fabrication need to be avoided. These terms imply that the client and therapist know the "facts" of a situation, facts that represent an immutable reality and demand certain consequences.

Language suggests choice by implying a sense that reality is something that happens interactionally and may be interpreted differently. The therapist can communicate this concept by talking about perceptions, opinions, beliefs, and appearances. The therapist can discuss what will "work," be "useful," be "productive," "fit," rather than the "right or perfect" solution, which implies no room for alternatives.

When labelling extrasession prescriptions, language is even more important. Consider what happens when the word "homework" is used with a school dropout or with someone who feels homework was a forced behavior in school. This term stimulates resistance immediately and thus suggests an attempt on the part of the therapist to force compliance. On the other hand, consider the person who believes that homework is the an efficient way to learn. Many teachers and professionals, for example, may view the idea of homework as quite practical. They are anxious to comply with the task. Extrasession labelling and prescriptions must be congruent with the client's perception of how change occurs. These extrasession tasks may be called "prescriptions," "homework," "tasks," "assignments," "chores," "experiences," "exercises," "experiments," and so on. The prescriptions may be given with more or less structure, more or less input from the client, and more or less flexibility.

The second factor that can be used to increase compliance and attribution of change to self is called personalism. Personalism refers to the idea of not stating the homework in a way that makes the clients feel coerced. Clients are more likely to feel coerced when they believe they are being personally directed (i.e. commanded or demanded) by the therapist. The therapist can avoid this problem by talking about the action needed to respond to the situation. The therapist might say, "This problem requires that you . . ." or "Part of the treatment for this problem involves _____ doing _____ at home." The therapist can also avoid this problem by softening statements such as, "I know" to "I think," "You're wrong about that" to "Let's take a look at what was just said," and "You should do . . ." to "It seems one choice is. . . ."

When giving a prescription, the therapist can emphasize the need to do certain things as a function of the situation. For example, when a couple begin treatment with a power struggle in the relationship, each partner perceives that the other is trying to force him or her to be a certain way or to do certain things. If the therapist then says they "must" do certain homework tasks, the pattern will be replicated with the therapist attempting to take control. In order to avoid a power struggle with a client-system, the locus of power must be shifted away from individual members and the therapist.

Contracting approaches accomplish this goal by shifting the power to the contract. The contract diffuses this power struggle by placing control in the mutually developed contract. By giving control to a mutually agreed upon contract, the partners believe they created control for themselves. An "external" system is now in control. Many systems of therapy rely on this principle. The therapist is seen as implementing a program, system, technique, and so on—not as imposing his or her own will on the client.

The degree of implicitness versus explicitness is the third variable. An implicit prescription produces greater compliance and self-attribution. An example of an implicit form of prescription is the Rogerian technique of reflective listening. Although it may appear that the therapist is exercising little control with this technique, the content of the material reflected back to the client and the way in which the material is reflected is indeed a form of control, albeit indirect.

In summary, the therapist does not want to increase the resistance of the client because this condition will be perceived as an attempt at forced compliance. The resistance of the client will be reduced if the client's sense of freedom is enhanced (e.g., the therapist offers several alternatives), and the degree of threat is reduced (e.g., the therapist accepts the client's pace).

RESISTANCE TO HOMEWORK

Homework compliance is a good predictor of commitment to change. When homework is not performed or is not successful, three strategies may be employed. The first is to process the homework in order to make explicit the forces that sabotaged it. In some cases, one partner does not believe the other will change so he or she does not follow through. In other cases, one partner will be feeling so resentful or angry that failure is certain. The reasons are often varied. Explanations may reside in the individual, in the interactional system, or in the intergenerational system (Weeks, 1989). The exploration of the meaning of change to the system may then free the client(s) to move forward. L'Abate et al. (1975) have also developed a method of dealing with resistance which may be useful with many couples. This method is a structured program on confronting change, which focuses the system on the meaning of change for them and how this meaning prevents the change from occurring.

When attempts at homework have failed repeatedly and the in-office sessions are stalled, it might be an appropriate time to try some paradoxical techniques (Weeks & L'Abate, 1982). The first strategy to be used is what Weeks and L'Abate (1982) call negative consequences of change. This involves asking the client-system to describe what kinds of negative consequences would result from making the kinds of changes that have been stated as desirable. The therapist then poses each positive change from the clients perspective in a negative light.

For example, conflict resolution homework might have been given to a couple. When their work fails, the couple would be asked to describe what would be negative about *not* fighting. The client(s) would probably say they would just "feel better," which is not really a response to the question. The therapist would challenge this statement with a rebuttal. For example, he or she might say, "It seems the only way to be close is to fight. Without it there might be nothing between you. Being really close might be too threatening for both of you at an unconscious level." The point of this strategy is to get the client(s) to resist *not* changing by pointing out the danger and in extreme cases the impossibility of change.

The second strategy is to shift to other paradoxical techniques, such as symptom prescription and restraint (Weeks & L'Abate, 1982). These strategies are specifically designed to turn resistance against itself and are beyond the scope of this paper. They have been described extensively elsewhere (Weeks, 1991; Weeks & L'Abate, 1982).

CONCLUSION

The change that is discussed and practiced in the session must extend beyond the therapist's office. In order to facilitate this change, the therapist may choose to assign homework. Homework involves doing something on a prescribed basis that is systematically laid out and designed to achieve a particular therapeutic goal. Homework assignments should grow from the sessions in an organic fashion. Many examples of homework can be found in the literature, but it works best to develop assignments that are tailored for each couple and developed collaboratively. Given this fact, standard assignments are usually not indicated. We may use other assignments as guides, but we should not be limited by them. Giving homework is a therapeutic skill just like any other. Knowledge and experience combine to contribute to more effective, successful, and appropriately timed experiences for the couple.

References

Abramson, L.Y., & Alloy, L.B. (1981). Depression, nondepression, and cognitive illusions: Reply to Schwartz. *Journal of Experimental Psychology: General, 110,* 436–447.

Abroms, M. (1981). Family therapy in a biomedical context. *Journal of Marital and Family Therapy, 7,* 385–390.

Alberti, R.E. & Emmons, M.L. (1983). *Your perfect right: A guide to assertive living.* San Luis Obispo, CA: Impact Publishers.

Alexander, J., & Parsons, B. (1982). *Functional family therapy.* Monterey, CA: Brooks, Cole.

Alloy, LB., & Abramson, L.Y. (1979). Judgment of contingency in depressed and non-depressed students: Sadder but wiser? *Journal of Experimental Psychology: General, 108,* 441–485.

American Psychiatric Association. (1987). *Diagnostic and statistical manual of mental disorders, third edition, revised.* Washington DC: APA Press.

Andolfi, M. (1979). Redefinition in family therapy. *American Journal of Family Therapy, 7,* 5–15.

Andolfi, M. (1980). *Family therapy: An interactional approach.* New York: Plenum Press.

Aponte, H., & Van Deusen, J. (1981). Structural family therapy. In A. Gurman & D. Kniskern (Eds.), *Handbook of family therapy* (vol. I). New York: Brunner/Mazel.

Ascher, L., Bowers, M., & Schotte, M. (1985). A review of data from controlled case studies and experiments evaluating the clinical efficacy of paradoxical intention. In G. Weeks (Ed.) *Promoting change through paradoxical therapy.* Homewood, Dow-Jones IL: Homewood, Ill.

Bandler, R., & Grinder, J. (1975). *The structure of magic.* Palo Alto, CA: Science & Behavior Books, Inc.

Bandler, R., & Grinder, J. (1982). *Reframing: Neuro-linguistic programming and the transformation of meaning.* Moab, UT: Real People Press.

Bateson, G. (1979). *Mind and nature. A necessary unity.* New York: Bantam.

Beck, A. (1976). *Cognitive therapy and the emotional disorder.* New York: International Universities Press.

Beck, A. (1988). *Love is never enough.* New York: Harper & Row.

Beisser, A. (1979). The paradoxical theory of change. In J. Fagan & I. Shepherd (Eds.), *Gestalt therapy now* (pp. 110–116). New York: Harper & Row.

Berman, E. (1982). The individual interview as a treatment technique in conjoint therapy. *The American Journal of Family Therapy, 10,* 27–37.

Berman, E., Lief, H., & Williams, A. (1981). A model of marital interaction. In M.

Scholevar (Ed.), *The handbook of marriage and marital therapy* (pp. 3–34). New York: S. P. Medical and Scientific Books.

Bernal, G., & Barker, J. (1979). Toward a metacommunication framework of couples intervention. *Family Process, 18,* 293–302.

Bowen, M. (1972). The use of theory in clinical practice. In J. Haley (Ed.), *Changing families* (pp. 159–192). New York: Grune & Stratton.

Bowen, M. (1978). *Family theory in clinical practice.* New York: Jason Aronson.

Bugental, J. (1987). *The art of psychotherapy.* New York: W. W. Norton.

Bulman, R.J., & Wortman, C.B. (1977). Attributions of blame and coping in the "real world": Severe accident victims react to their lot. *Journal of Personality and Social Psychology, 35,* 351–363.

Burns, D. (1980). *Feeling good: The new mood therapy.* New York: Signet.

Burton, A. (Ed.). (1976). *What makes behavioral change possible.* New York: Brunner/Mazel.

Doherty, W., Colangelo, N., Green, A., & Hoffman, G. (1985). Emphases of the major family therapy models: A family FIRO analysis. *Journal of Marital and Family Therapy, 11,* 299–303.

Duhl, J., & Duhl, P. (1981). Integrative family therapy. In A. Gurman & D. Kniskern (Eds.), *Handbook of family therapy,* vol. I (pp. 483–516). New York: Brunner/Mazel.

Ellis, A. (1962). *Reason and emotion in psychotherapy.* New York: Lyle Stuart.

Ellis, A. (1987). The impossibility of achieving consistently good mental health. *American Psychologist, 42,* 364–375.,

Ellis, A., & Harper, R. (1961a). *A guide to rational living.* Hollywood, CA: Wilshire Books.

Ellis, A., & Harper, R. (1961b). *A guide to successful marriage.* North Hollywood, CA: Wilshire Books.

Epstein, N. (1982). Cognitive therapy with couples. *The American Journal of Family Therapy, 10,* 5–16.

Epstein, N. (1986). Cognitive marital therapy: A multilevel assessment & intervention. *Journal of Rational Emotive Therapy, 4,* 68–81.

Feldman, L. (1982). Dysfunctional marital conflict: An integrative interpersonal-intrapsychic model. *Journal of Marital and Family Therapy, 8,* 417–428.

Fleuridas, C., Nelson, S., & Rosenthal, D. (1986). The evolution of circular questions: Training family therapists. *Journal of Marital and Family Therapy, 12,* 113–128.

Fraser, J. (Ed.). (1984). Special issue on integration/disintegration (special issue). *Journal of Strategic and Systemic Therapies, 3.*

Green, R., & Kolevzon, M. (1982). Three approaches to family therapy: A study of convergence and divergence. *Journal of Marital and Family Therapy, 8,* 39–50.

Greenberg, L., & Johnson, S. (1986a). Affect in marital therapy. *Journal of Marital and Family Therapy, 12,* 1–10.

Greenberg, L., & Johnson, S. (1986b). When to evoke emotion and why: Process diagnosis in couples therapy. *Journal of Marital and Family Therapy, 12,* 19–23.

Greenwald, A.G. (1980). The totalitarian ego: Fabrication and revision of personal history. *American Psychologist, 35,* 603–618.

Grunbaum, H., & Chasin, R. (1978). Reframing reconsidered: The beneficial effects of a pathological label. *Family Process, 17,* 449–456.

Gurman, A., & Kniskern, D. (Eds.). (1981a). *Handbook of family therapy* (vol. I). New York: Brunner/Mazel.

Gurman, A., & Kniskern, D. (1981b). Family therapy outcome research: Knowns and unknowns. In A. Gurman & D. Kniskern (Eds.), *Handbook of family therapy*, vol. I (pp. 742–776). New York: Brunner/Mazel.

Haley, J. (1973). *Uncommon therapy: The psychiatric techniques of Milton H. Erickson*. New York: Ballantine.

Haley, J. (1976). *Problem-solving therapy*. San Francisco: Jossey-Bass.

Hatcher, C. (1978). Intrapersonal and interpersonal models: Blending gestalt and family therapies. *Journal of Marriage and Family Counseling, 4*, 63–68.

Heller, J. (1987). A beginner's guide to the first family interview. *American Journal of Family Therapy, 15*, 291–304.

Hof, L., & Miller, W. (1981). *Marriage enrichment*. Bowie, MD: Robert & Brady Co.

Hoffman, L. (1981). *Foundations of family therapy*. New York: Basic Books.

Jacobson, N. (1981). Behavioral marital therapy. In A. Gurman & D. Kniskern (Eds.), *Handbook of family therapy*, vol. I. New York: Brunner/Mazel.

James, W. (1907). *Pragmatism*. New York: World Publishing.

Jessee, E., & L'Abate, L. (1985). Paradoxical treatment of depression in married couples. In L. L'Abate (Ed.), *The handbook of family psychology and therapy*. (pp. 1128–1151). Homewood, IL: The Dorsey Press.

Jones, W. (1986). Frame cultivation: Helping new meanings take root in families. *American Journal of Family Therpay, 14*, 57–68.

Kaslow, F. (1981). A diaclectic approach to family therapy and practice: Selectivity and synthesis. *Journal of Marital and Family Therapy, 7*, 345–351.

Kelly, G. (1955). *The psychology of personal constructs, Vol. 1, A history of personality*. New York: W. W. Norton.

Kelley, H. (1983). Love & commitment. In H. Kelley et al., *Close relationships*. New York: W.H. Freeman & Co.

Kerr, M. (1981). Family systems: Theory and practice. In A. Gurman & D. Kniskern (Eds.), *Handbook of family therapy*, vol.I. (pp. 226–266). New York: Brunner/Mazel.

L'Abate, L. (1975). A positive approach to marital and family intervention. In L. Wolberg & M. Aronson (Eds.), *Group therapy 1975—An overview*. New York: Stratton Intercontinental Medical Books.

L'Abate, L. (1977). *Enrichment: Structural interventions with couples, families and groups*. Washington DC: University Press of America.

L'Abate, L. (1986). *Systematic family therapy*. New York: Brunner/Mazel.

L'Abate, L., et al. (1975). *Enrichment programs for the family life cycle*. Atlanta, GA: Social Research Laboratories.

L'Abate, L., Ganahl, G., & Hansen, J. (1986). *Methods of family therapy*. Englewood Cliffs, NJ: Prentice Hall.

L'Abate, L., & L'Abate, B. (1977). *Help for troubled marriages*. John Knox: Atlanta, GA.

L'Abate, L., & McHenry, S. (1983). *Handbook of marital interventions*. New York: Grune & Stratton.

L'Abate, L., & Samples, G. (1983). Intimacy letters: Invariable prescriptions for closeness-avoidant couples. *Family Therapy, 10*, 37–45.

Lazarus, R.S. (1983). The costs and benefits of denial. In S. Breznitz (Ed.), *Denial of stress*. New York: International Universities Press.

Lebow, J. (1984). On the nature of integrating approaches to family therapy. *Journal of Marital and Family Therapy, 10,* 127–138.

Lerner, H. Goldhor. (1989). *The dance of anger.* New York: Harper Collins.

Levant, R. (1984). *Family therapy: A comprehensive overview.* Englewood Cliffs, NJ: Prentice Hall.

Lewinsohn, P.M., Mischel, W., Chaplin, W., & Barton, R. (1980). Social competence and depression: The role of illusory self-perceptions. *Journal of Abnormal Psychology, 89,* 203–212.

Mack, R. (1989). Spouse abuse—A dyadic approach. In G. Weeks (Ed.), *Treating couples: The intersystem model of the Marriage Council of Philadelphia.* New York: Brunner/Mazel.

McGoldrick, M., & Gerson, R. (1985). *Genograms in family assessment.* New York: W.W. Norton.

Miller, D.T., & Ross, M. (1975). Self-serving biases in the attribution of causality: Fact or fiction? *Psychological Bulletin, 82,* 213–225.

Millon, T. (1981). *Disorders of personality: DSM-III, Axis II.* New York: Wiley.

Minuchin, S. (1974). *Families and family therapy.* Cambridge, MA: Harvard University Press.

Minuchin, S., & Fishman, H. (1981). *Family therapy techniques.* Cambridge, MA: Harvard University Press.

Napier, A. (1978). The rejection-intrusion pattern: A central family dynamic. *Journal of Marriage & Family Counseling, 4,* 5–12.

√Napier, A. (1990). *The fragile bond.* New York: Harper & Row.

Nichols, M. (1984). *Family therapy: Concepts and methods.* New York: Marber Press.

O'Leary, K., & Turkewitz, H. (1978). Marital therapy from a behavioral perspective. In T. Paolino & B. McCrady (Eds.), *Marriage & marital therapy* (pp. 260–297). New York: Brunner/Mazel.

Palazzoli, M., Boscolo, L., Cecchin, M., & Prata, G. (1978). *Paradox and counter-paradox.* New York: Jason Aronson.

Penn, P. (1982). Circular questioning. *Family Process, 12,* 267–279.

√Pierce, R., Nichols, M., & DuBrin, J. (1983). *Emotional expression in psychotherapy.* New York: Gardner Press, Inc.

Protinsky, H., & Quinn, W. (1981). Paradoxical marital therapy with symptom triangulation. *Family Therapy, 8,* 136–140.

The Random House college dictionary. (1975). New York: Random House, Inc.

Rubin, Z. (1973). *Liking and loving.* New York: Holt, Rhinehart & Winston.

Sager, C. (1976). *Marriage contracts and couples therapy.* New York: Brunner/Mazel.

Sager, C., & Hunt, B. (1979). *Intimate partners.* New York: McGraw-Hill.

Satir, V. (1967). *Conjoint family therapy.* Palo Alto, CA: Science & Behavioral Books.

Scharff, D., & Scharff, J. (1987). *Object relations family therapy.* New York: Aronson.

Sheldon, J., & Ackerman, J. (1974). *Homework in counseling and psychotherapy.* Springfield, IL: Charles C Thomas.

Sloan, S., & L'Abate, L. (1985). Intimacy. In L. L'Abate (Ed.), *Handbook of family psychology therapy* (pp. 405–431). Homewood, IL: Dorsey Press.

Stanton, M. (1981). An integrative structural/strategic approach to family therapy. *Journal of Marital and Family Therapy*, 7, 427–439.

Stanton, M., Todd, T., & Associates. (1982). *The family therapy of drug addiction*. New York: Guilford.

Sternberg, R. (1986a). A triangular theory of love. *Psychological Review*, 93, 119–135.

Sternberg, R. (1986b). Love, sex, & intimacy. *Psychological Review*, 93, 119–135.

Strong, S., & Claiborn, C. (1982). *Change through interaction: Social psychological processes of counseling and psychotherapy*. New York: John Wiley.

Stuart, R. (1980). *Helping couples change*. New York: Guilford Press.

Taylor, S.E. (1983). Adjustment to threatening events. *American Psychologist*, 38, 1161–1173.

Tennen, H., Affleck, G., Allen, D.A., McGrade, B.J., & Ratzan, S. (in press). Causal attributions and coping with insulin-dependent diabetes. *Basic and applied social psychology*.

Tennen, H., Eron, J., & Rohrbaugh, M. (1991). Paradox in context. In G. Weeks (Rev. Ed.), *Promoting change through paradoxical therapy* (pp. 187–214). New York: Brunner/Mazel.

Tennen, H., & Herzberger, S. *Depression, self-esteem, and the absence of self-protective attributional biases*. Manuscript submitted for publication.

Tiger, L. (1979). *Optimism: The biology of hope*. New York: Simon & Schuster.

Viaro, M. (1980). Case report: Smuggling family therapy through. *Family Process*, 19, 35–44.

Wachtel, E., & Wachtel, P. (1986). *Family dynamics in individual psychotherapy*. New York: Guilford.

Warburton, J., & Alexander, J. (1985). The family therapist: What does one do? In L. L'Abate (Ed.), *The handbook of family psychology and therapy*, vol. II (pp. 1318–1343). Homewood, IL: Dorsey Press.

Watzlawick, P., Beavin, J., & Jackson, D. (1967). *Pragmatics of human communication*. New York: W. W. Norton.

Watzlawick, P., Weakland, J., & Fisch, R. (1974). *Change: Principles of problem formation and problem resolution*. New York: W. W. Norton.

Weber, T., McKeever, J., & McDaniel, S. (1985). A beginner's guide to the problem-oriented first family interview. *Family Process*, 24, 357–364.

Weeks, G. (1977). Toward a dialectical approach to intervention. *Human Development*, 20, 277–292.

Weeks, G. (1985). Individual-system dialectic. *American Journal of Family Therapy*, 14, 5–12.

Weeks, G. (1989). An intersystem approach to treatment. In G. Weeks (Ed.), *Treating couples: The intersystem model of the Marriage Council of Philadelphia* (pp. 317–340). New York: Brunner/Mazel.

Weeks, G. (1990). Paradox. In J. Zeig & W. Munion (Eds.), *What is psychotherapy?* (pp. 262–265). San Francisco: Jossey-Bass.

Weeks, G. (1991). (Ed.). *Promoting change through paradoxical therapy*. New York: Brunner/Mazel.

Weeks, G., & Hof, L. (Eds.). (1987). *Integrating sex and marital therapy*. New York: Brunner/Mazel.

Weeks, G., & L'Abate, L. (1982). *Paradoxical psychotherapy: Theory and practice with individuals, couples, and families.* New York: Brunner/Mazel.

Weiss, R., Hops, H., & Patterson G. (1973). A framework for conceptualizing marital conflict: A technology for altering it, some data for evaluating it. In L. Hamerlynck, L. Handy, & E. Mash (Eds.), *Behavior change: Methodology, concepts, and practice.* Champaign, IL: Research Press.

Name Index

Subject Index